THE CA

By the same author:

CALVIN AND THE CALVINISTS
THE BEGINNINGS

THE CALLINGS

*The Gospel
in the World*

PAUL HELM

THE BANNER OF TRUTH TRUST

THE BANNER OF TRUTH TRUST
3 Murrayfield Road, Edinburgh EH 12 6EL
PO Box 621, Carlisle, Pennsylvania 17013, USA

★

© Paul Helm 1987
First published 1987
ISBN 0 85151 512 6

★

Typeset in 10½/12pt Linotron Plantin
At The Spartan Press Ltd, Lymington, Hants
Printed and bound in Great Britain by
Hazell Watson & Viney Limited,
Member of the BPCC Group,
Aylesbury, Bucks

Contents

[v]

To
Philip and Marjorie

Introduction

It is sometimes forgotten that most Christians are not in 'full-time Christian service' and are not intended to be. They are called to be faithful Christians in other ways. Among evangelical Christians in particular there has grown up the idea that a Christian who is doing an 'ordinary job' cannot be a Christian in the fullest sense. The assumption behind such a view is that the sum and substance of the Christian life is 'witness' and that those who are not constantly employed in 'witnessing' are only shadow-Christians. And so Christians are led to believe that the first question to be asked about their life and work is not whether it is worthwhile, satisfying and useful, but whether it provides them with the opportunity to witness.

It is likely that such an attitude, though well-intentioned, in fact produces a great deal of harm. Paradoxically, although the advocates of such a view of the Christian life intend to promote the witness of Christians, they devalue it. Sometimes, as a result of being confronted with this attitude, young people become accustomed to regard 'full-time Christian service' as the only fitting occupation for a faithful Christian. As a result they feel pressured, if not by others then by themselves, into thinking that the only worthwhile life in God's sight is a career in some church-related activity. How else does one explain the growth of para-church ministries in the twentieth century?

What produces the views described is an attitude

among Christians that can best be described as split-mindedness. Christians have become accustomed to think of themselves as having a 'spiritual life' which is sharply distinct from the every-day life in the family, and from work and leisure. A 'spiritual life' is a life of prayer and watchfulness, of Bible-reading and church-going. As a result of this distortion, instead of the Christian life being thought of as an integrated whole, it is artifically broken up into compartments which have little or nothing to do with one another. The 'vertical' dimension of a person's life with God seems unrelated and unrelatable to the 'horizontal' dimension of his life on planet Earth. It is as if Christian responsibility ceases at the church porch, as if the Christian gospel has nothing to do with the pavement outside and the roads and motorways beyond.

There are other evangelical Protestants who understand the Christian life mainly in cultural terms. They see the Reformation, for example, not so much as the rediscovery of the biblical gospel but as a break with the social and cultural hold of mediaeval Catholicism. It provides, in their view, the elements of what is called a 'Christian life and world view'. The Christian's life of Bible-reading, prayer and self-examination, and missionary and evangelistic endeavour, is dismissed as 'pietism'.

These extreme positions are not only found within today's church. At times during her history sections of the church have been so much impressed with the 'eternal' side of the faith that they have attempted to cut themselves off from the world and its influences. The monastic movement of the Middle Ages and the Anabaptist wing of the Reformation are different expressions of this attitude. More recently, at least since the influence of the eighteenth-century Enlightenment has been felt, many in the church have placed increasing emphasis upon the 'this worldly' character of the faith, the present social ob-

[x]

ligations and political opportunities. The excesses of 'liberation theology' are only the latest expression of this attitude. So great has this emphasis become that there is the danger of understanding the Christian faith wholly in such terms.

But such splits in Christian mentality, whether occurring within Protestant evangelicalism or farther afield, seem to be entirely foreign to the New Testament. The apostles have a great deal to say, as Christ himself had, about the tensions in the Christian's life, the tension between the flesh and the spirit, and between present responsibilities and the glory that is to come. But the picture they paint is of such men and women living one life before God, not two or more lives in opposition and conflict one with the other. They seem to be able to preserve a balance between the 'vertical' and the 'horizontal' and entirely to avoid thinking in these ways.

This book tries to offer a way of healing this split and of rectifying the unbalanced attitude to the ministry which is partly its cause and partly its effect.

The place to begin, as far as Christian responsibility is concerned, is where the New Testament begins, with the work of God's grace through Christ in the life of the individual. At the heart of true Christian experience and responsibility is the Christian message of new life to people who are dead before God – a new life which first requires reconciliation with God through Christ, and then the renewing and sanctifying influences of Christ's Spirit. It must be emphasised that any attempts at overcoming split-mindedness, at reintegrating the thinking and responsibilities of Christian people, must begin at this point and, in a sense, never get beyond it. They must not lose sight of this basic relationship with God.

The Bible conceives of this relationship in many different ways. It is sonship, reconciliation, a new birth, a resurrection, a new creation, a being begotten again. It is also a *calling*, the voice of God impressing itself on the mind and conscience as the truth of the biblical message concerning Jesus Christ is received. And this call is effective. It is not a mere general announcement to all and sundry that Jesus saves, important as such an announcement is. It is God bringing an individual to the place where he is enabled to respond to Christ in repentance and faith. This is the call which brings a response. It is this call that makes a person a Christian and keeps him one. Any proposals for Christian service which deny this foundation truth, which pay mere lip-service to it, or which fail to give it the vital prominence which it has in Scripture, cannot be authentically Christian.[1]

While the effective call of God by grace must always be at the centre of Christian thinking, it is at precisely this point that there is a tendency to falter, to fail to follow through to the rest of the biblical teaching. For how does the Christian integrate the remainder of his life into the new life he receives at conversion? Conversion according to the New Testament is such a radical affair that it seems that everything else must be over-ruled by it. What does the second birth have to do with a man's first birth, or the new life he has in Christ with his daily routine? What does resurrection in Christ have to do with getting up each morning? Not very much, Christians are taught to think, and so the seeds of split-mindedness are sown.

But this is to forget that the Bible, and especially the New Testament, teaches not only that the Christian is effectively called by divine grace but that he is called in other complementary senses. It teaches that the whole of a person's situation in life as the converting grace of God comes to him constitutes his *calling*. It is not an accident

[1] The elements of this calling have been considered in an earlier book, *The Beginnings* (1986), to which this present book is a sequel.

[xii]

that a person is where he is, and like he is, when he is converted, and provided that he is not engaged in a course of life which is intrinsically sinful, he is to regard that situation as God's calling to him. So, at least, Paul teaches the Corinthian believers (*1 Corinthians 7*). Nowadays the idea of a calling or vocation, where it is used at all, is limited to special occupations such as nursing or social work. But the biblical view is that any lawful occupation may be a calling and more than this, that the whole of a person's life is a calling from God. God is *in* it. It has His blessing. It is the product of His providential ruling. And the Christian is to live his life in the belief that God continues to call him to be where he is, to use his gifts to the full. Such an idea was prominent at the Reformation, but is now largely forgotten.

But there is more. For the New Testament also teaches that the believer is *called to freedom*. He is called out of the bondage of sin and he is relieved of the daunting responsibility of keeping the intricate and demanding requirements of the Old Testament ceremonial law. Christ has made him free. And yet such freedom is not anarchic. The Christian is not free to live as he pleases. The freedom is structured, structured by the moral law of God and by the inspiration and example of Christ who humbled Himself and became obedient to death, even the death of the cross. Many elements enter into this structure; responsibilities in the family, at work, to the state and in wider society. Integrating these into one Christian life is a problem, many problems. But it is to such whole-hearted and whole-minded service that the Christian is called.

Yet the Christian's calling does not end here. He is *called to a kingdom and glory* (*1 Thess. 2.12*), to a heavenly kingdom. His horizon is not bounded by this life, important and demanding and enjoyable though it is, but it takes in the life to come. In this sense the Christian life is a *heavenly calling*, a life which will endure to the life to come. And the glory to come is not separate from the life being lived now. It is its consummation, when the dross will be refined away and the Christian will stand complete in Christ, having the mind of Christ, a mind whose formation is begun on earth and only completed at the end-time. It is important to stress the continuity. If sinless perfection and Christ-likeness are only experienced in the life to come, they are the end-points of a process. Human character is re-formed under the influence of the indwelling Spirit as the Christian engages faithfully in the calling to which he has been assigned. The character, gifts and aptitudes formed and developed under these conditions will be consummated in heaven. As the Son of God has taken into glory what He learned on earth as the Godman, as He carried His wounds there, so the believer will take with him the character formed below, refined and made perfect in heaven.

It is in terms of these four callings – God's effective call in conversion, God's calling in life, God's call to freedom and God's heavenly calling – that the case for the Christian's responsibility to integrate his thinking and living before God is made. It is hoped that by staying as closely as this to the teaching of the New Testament the abstract theorising which so often plagues discussion of these matters even among Christians will be avoided. For one of the important matters that emerges from a consideration of the New Testament is that there is no 'party line'. As each person is different so his or her life-situation is different and calls for a different application of the revealed truth of God.

It is freely acknowledged therefore that such an attempt to provide in writing an attempt to integrate the Christian life is only a beginning. A book or study such as this has limited value. No book ought to presume to provide all the answers, but at most to set in motion courses of thought and reflection that a person can take further for himself and which will lead to authentic Christian action. Such, at least, is the aim of this book.

1: The Call that Brings a Response

The proclamation of God's saving grace in Christ to all who will hear it is central to the Christian church's mission to the world. The making known of this good news is intended to be indiscriminate, for it is to any and every person without respect to his race, or creed, or personal circumstances. By means of preaching, and the re-production of preaching in literature, tapes and radio, this call to come to Christ for mercy is made throughout the earth each day.

Christ Himself taught that the hearing of this call is necessary in order for a person to become a Christian (*Matt. 13:1–23*), and the apostles echo His teaching (*Rom. 10:14*). Paul says that faith – the faith that saves, that unites a person to Christ and which brings pardon and righteousness – comes by hearing, the hearing of the Word of God (*Rom. 10:17*). But not all who hear the Word of God are saved. This is obvious from the evidence of history, and it is also what is seen in the diverse responses to Christ's own teaching and to the preaching of the apostles. When the same announcement of the good news is made some are hostile to what they hear, others are indifferent, and still others receive what they hear and trust Christ (*Acts 4:1–4*).

Beginning with Peter's sermon on the Day of Pentecost (*Acts 2:1–47*), the reaction to Christian preaching has never been total acceptance, nor complete rejection. So when Paul preached to the Epicureans and Stoics at

Athens (*Acts 17*) some of them mocked him when he mentioned the resurrection of the dead, some said that they would like to hear him on another occasion, while others became believers (*Acts 17:34*). The apostles cannot have been surprised at this, for there was a similar division when Christ preached the gospel.

THE TWO CALLINGS

What made the difference? What explains the division between those who accept and those who reject the preaching of the good news? It is tempting to look for an explanation of the difference in the way we explain other differences between people, in terms of class, or occupation, or age or personality. But the evidence provided by the New Testament does not lend any support to such an approach, for an examination of the lives of those who became Christians reveals a great variety of backgrounds, not one common factor. Some Christians were rich (*Luke 19:1–10*) and some were poor (*1 Cor. 1:26*). Some were free (*Gal. 3:28*), others were slaves (*1 Pet. 2:18*). There were young and old, men and women, Jews and Gentiles. Besides, there is not the least suggestion that the apostles *thought* that their message was for a particular group or type, nor that they believed that what they said was tailored to be more acceptable to some than to others.

So what makes the difference? Why is it that some believe the good news and some do not? What explanation does Scripture itself offer?

Scripture teaches that besides the general 'call', the preaching of the gospel to all alike, there is a further 'call', a call from God which itself brings a response from those who are called, the response of repentance and faith in Christ and of sincere obedience to what God requires. Not all who are called are called in this sense. Not all who are called by the general preaching of the gospel are called by God in such a way as to ensure the appropriate response.

This further call, the call that brings a response, comes directly from God. It is true that the general call of the gospel is from God as well, since God authorises and empowers men to preach, and they speak at His command. But the further, inward call is more immediately the work of God. One way that the New Testament has of making this clear is to say that while a preacher or teacher can teach the gospel to others, and encourage and warn them, *only* God by His grace can secure the acceptance of the good news. No matter how eloquent or clear or winsome a human preacher may be, what he says will not, by itself, bring hearers to faith in Christ. God alone can do such a thing. No doubt with Christ's teaching in the parable of the sower in mind, Paul reminded the Corinthians that while one man may sow the seed, and another man may water, none but God can make the seed spring to life and bear fruit (*1 Cor. 3:6*).

God's effective call, the call which brings a response, is more than the general call of the gospel through preaching. And yet it would be misleading to leave the impression that when a person is converted through the preaching of the good news, when he is called by God, he experiences two separate calls, one from the preacher and another from God. It is not so. God's direct call does not involve the person who is called in receiving *another* message, through a vision or voice or an inner prompting, besides the good news that he hears in common with all the others who hear it. There is one message of good news, exactly the same for all. A person is not converted by receiving an additional 'secret message'.

But if the call from God which secures a response is not an additional teaching, what is it? It is the activity of God who makes a person receptive and responsive to the truth

[3]

which he hears. The inward 'call' is not more information, it is the clearing and renewing of the mind of the one who hears so that he understands the good news. It is also the removing of the prejudice which all people have to the authority of God, and it is the renewing of the will in order that the response of faith and obedience may be made as the good news is announced.

For illustration, consider the difference between a skilled engineer and a novice. Both may listen to the idling of an engine and the skilled engineer may at once be able to tell what is wrong, what is causing the vibration or uneven-ness. Yet both the engineer and the novice hear the same sounds. What is a puzzle to one is immediately clear to the other. The difference is due to the training and experience of the engineer. But in the case of the *effectual* call of a sinner by God, the difference is not that the one called has certain aptitudes or abilities which the one who is not called lacks. Emphatically not. The difference is due to divine grace alone. And this grace shows itself in a difference in appreciation, a difference which is brought about by a change in the person's innermost dispositions and attitudes, a change which only God can make.

Hence, in the conversion of a person through the proclamation of the Christian good news, there is a two-fold call. There is the general call of the gospel through preaching and there is the particular, effective call of God working a change in a person's inner character to make him appreciative of the gospel and responsive to it.

If this double sense of 'call' is borne in mind then certain parts of the New Testament which are otherwise difficult to understand, and which may even seem to be contradictory, become clear. When Paul, writing to the Corinthians, says 'But unto them which are called, both Jews and Greeks, Christ the power of God, and the wisdom of God' (*1 Cor. 1:24*), he is referring to their effectual calling, their calling by God through the preaching of the good news and their divinely-empowered response to it. That empowering took no account of wisdom or natural birth, and it was certainly not *because of* such matters. Paul says that, in general, God had called the poor and foolish among men in order to show that coming to Christ was nothing to boast about. It was certainly not due to greater natural intelligence or insight.

On the other hand, consider Christ's words 'Many are called, but few are chosen' (*Matt. 20:16*). Here Christ is referring to the general call of the gospel, and teaching that while many are called outwardly through preaching, comparatively few are called effectually, are 'chosen'. So Christ uses 'chosen' here to describe the effective activity of God in conversion, while Paul uses 'called'. And yet the contrast is not as great as it may seem, for Paul also, in the passage already considered, writes of the 'called' as those whom God has chosen (*1 Cor. 1:27*). And clearly the idea of choice, God's choice, is very appropriate to describe the unilateral, effective way in which God makes His grace known to sinners in their conversion.

The fact that the effective call (or choice) of God is not a separate message or revelation from God, but that it accompanies the exposition of the gospel of grace in preaching, underlines the fact that conversion always occurs in circumstances in which the good news is made known. No one is converted who is ignorant of the way of salvation through God's mercy in Christ. How could they be? To suppose such a thing would mean that such a person knew nothing at all about God's mercy in Christ. But how could they go to God for mercy if they knew nothing about God's mercy, and had no idea that they were warranted to go to God in their need? A person may be prepared by God for conversion at a time when he is ignorant of the good news. Such a person may come to

[5]

experience an unaccountable need, a profound dissatisfaction with himself, an unnamed longing which he is unable fully to understand, or to satisfy, until Christ is preached to him and he comes to Christ for mercy. But this is unusual. Ordinarily it is as the good news is proclaimed that all the phases of effectual calling take place.

Why, in conveying His mercy to sinful people, does God work effectively, unilaterally, in the way described? Because there is no other way for Him to work. Such an answer is not meant to reflect unfavourably upon God, as though He was limited in power and goodness. It is not so much a comment on the power or goodness of God as upon the plight or need of mankind. Man's plight is such that to suppose that he could be encouraged or cajoled into the kingdom of God would be to mock him. People in need of God's mercy, with their faces turned away from Him, and in a condition which the New Testament describes as death (*Eph. 2:1*) and enmity (*Rom. 8.7*), will not respond even to the sweetest and most persuasive reasonings of God Himself until they are given strength to do so. The idea that people are neutral, and that they need someone or some influence to tip the balance in God's favour, betrays a deep misunderstanding of the spiritual condition of mankind. Sin makes men hostile to God. Sin *is* hostility to God. Unconverted people live in opposition to Him. The only way in which they can be changed is to be turned about, to be given new life or recreated. The New Testament does not hesitate to use such radical language – the language of creation, new birth and resurrection – to describe how a person is brought to Christ.

So while the call of the gospel through preaching is *general*, without restriction, in accordance with Christ's command to His servants to proclaim the good news in all the world, yet the inward, effectual call of God which makes the good news intelligible and acceptable, is *particular*. This effectual call does not come to classes of people as such, or to nations, but to individual people within classes or nations. This distinction between the general and the particular call applied equally well to Israel in the Old Testament era. And even if large numbers of people in a society become Christians at one and the same time it is not valid to infer from this that it has happened because they were somehow fitted or entitled to receive God's mercy.

The character of the effective call of God shows more clearly than anything else that salvation comes to individual men and women only as a result of God's mercy. When Paul preached at Athens (or Jesus preached in Galilee) why was it that some scoffingly rejected what he said and others received it? The explanation cannot be that God is not sufficiently powerful or wise effectively to call an Epicurean or a Stoic philosopher. Nor does the explanation lie in the fact that one person is naturally more inclined to be converted than another. Rather, conversion is explained by the fact that God sees fit to grant His saving grace.

Perhaps nothing highlights more clearly the *sovereignly merciful* character of the effective call than the fact that, while all need salvation, only some receive it. It could never be argued that people are converted because they deserve to be converted. If this were so why are not all converted, since all are equally needy?

Paul argues along these lines in Romans 9, where he discusses the case of Jacob and Esau. God had mercy on Jacob, while Esau was denied mercy. Paul shows that God's treatment of them cannot have been on account of anything either of them did, since God had determined how to act before either of them had been born. But if God had mercy on Jacob and rejected Esau, could He not have had mercy on both, or rejected both? Why did He not treat them alike? Paul gives the unanswerable reply that God chose to distribute His mercy in the way He did, and not in some other way, simply because He is God. It is His right to dispense mercy as He pleases because He has dominion over all his creation, and all that He does is based upon perfect wisdom.

So the effective call of God, the call which secures a response, is not due to human goodness or human preparedness of any kind which might be thought to predispose God to favour one individual instead of another. Conversion has its source not in any qualifications which a person may have, but in the eternal election of God. Paul brings this out vividly when writing to the Thessalonian church. He says that when they were converted the good news came powerfully to them because of God's prior choice of them. Because of this eternal choice, when the appropriate time came, God effectively called them as the good news was preached to them (*1 Thess. 1:4–7*).

EQUALITY BEFORE GOD

Not only does God not grant His mercy exclusively to one particular human group or class, the New Testament is also clear and emphatic that receiving the good news with penitence and faith does not require any special aptitude or ability. While God's mercy in Christ contains profound depths which the human mind cannot fully fathom (*Rom. 11:33*), nevertheless the good news of the gospel is simple and straightforward in its essentials. It does not require great cleverness to grasp it, though able men who have grasped it have found in it much food for thought, men of the calibre of Augustine of Hippo. And while faith in Christ has led some people to live amazing lives in which they devoted themselves to Christian learning, or to courageous missionary work, or to devoted service to the sick and dying, yet faith in Christ, while the product of divine grace, is nevertheless simple. A small child or an old person on the verge of death may have faith in Christ.

As Paul says, it is not as if, in order to become a Christian, a person has to engage in a spiritual search to locate Christ, to bring Him down from heaven. God is near to each one of us. As His word is proclaimed He is present. All that is required is that the person confesses Christ and believes in his heart that He is the divinely-appointed Saviour. Whoever calls on the name of the Lord shall be saved (*Rom. 10:13*).

This fact is both humbling and encouraging. It is humbling to any who may be inclined to think that they are well-qualified to become Christians. There is no such thing as being well-qualified to be a Christian. Becoming a Christian does not require a person to fill in an application form giving details of past education and experience. The only 'qualification' needed is the need of forgiveness and righteousness. Paradoxically, a person is qualified to come to Christ not by what he is or has achieved but by what he does not have and has failed to achieve. This is a humbling fact, a fact which has sent men away from Christ in sorrow, for example the rich young ruler who talked with Christ (*Luke 18:23*).

But if this fact is humbling it is also encouraging. If a person recognises his need of Christ he need lose no time in coming to Christ. For what should he wait? To become better qualified, a better person, more 'worthy' of Christ? Such ways of thinking, though natural, are twisted. They are natural because it is natural for sinful men to think of their relationship to God in terms of *doing*. But the good news of God's mercy in Christ is *free*. It is not for the doers but for the trusters, not for those who have confidence in their own abilities or attainments but for those who rely upon Christ. The fact that nothing is needed to qualify a person to come to Christ but only the need for Christ – and everyone has this need – is something which the mind of man finds impossible to take in until he is changed by divine grace. Grace shows men that their need, and God's mercy in Jesus, are perfectly matched.

What all this indicates is that Christians, as Christians, are equal with one another. They enjoy a God-given equality. For the effective grace of God in Christ which makes them Christians, comes to them not because they are specially qualified, but because of God's love for them, and that alone. So it is nonsense to suppose that one Christian is more of a Christian than another, or that one Christian has more need of God's grace to be saved than another. The jibe that all men are equal but that some are more equal than others, however true of the animals in George Orwell's *Animal Farm*, cannot be applied to Christians.

Yet the equality which all Christians enjoy needs to be clearly understood. The grains of sugar in a bag are all equal, but this kind of equality does not adequately convey the equality that all Christians have in Christ. The grains are separable and are lumped together in bags in a quite arbitrary way. But the equality which Christians have is better understood *organically*. It is the equality of cells in a living body rather than of inert and lifeless grains of sugar. The reason for this is that each Christian is united to Christ as his Head and Saviour. This is what Paul is teaching when he says that all believers are 'one in Christ Jesus' (*Gal. 3:28*). As regards their relationship to Christ each is in exactly the same position even though one may be a slave and another free, one a man and another a woman.

So while there is equality in Christ, equality of status

and relation, there is also difference. Paul is not saying that differences of age or sex or aptitude vanish when people become Christians. How could they vanish? How could becoming a Christian stop an old person from being old, or a woman from being a woman? So what Paul is saying is that, as regards a person's relation to God, God's grace to Christians is such that they cannot fail to be on an equal footing with one another, whatever the other differences among them might be.

But the New Testament portrayal of this equality is a fuller and richer one than the idea of cells in a body. It is the picture of the body and its limbs. Christ is the head of the body and believers are the limbs. Each limb is essential to the body, necessary for its proper functioning (*1 Cor. 12:14–24*). There are differences in function between Christians just as the different parts of the body perform different functions.

Given the fact of the fundamental equality of all believers in Christ, and the body of Christ as consisting of different limbs, differences between Christians can only be *functional*. There is no difference in status or hierarchy between Christians so that one group is essentially different from, or superior to, others. This would be a violation of the equality which all Christians have in Christ. The differences between Christians arise out of differences in gifts and abilities and opportunities, and these lead to different Christians performing different functions. Carrying out these different functions is to be characterised not by dominion but by service, as Paul taught (*2 Cor. 4:5*), clearly following Christ's own teaching in the Gospels (*Matt. 20:25–28*).

Sometimes the biblical idea of Christian diversity in unity, a diversity of function carried out in a spirit of service, has been exaggerated into that of a hierarchy uniquely gifted in virtue of ordination to perform and validate certain indispensable rites. At the other extreme diversity has been denied, with a great emphasis placed upon uniformity. Such an attitude was characteristic of certain aspects of mediaeval monasticism, the idea of a monastic brotherhood. Again, in a different historical situation, this attitude can be seen in the Anabaptist movement in which Christian equality took the form of communistic living.

The equality before God which, as we have seen, is an integral part of God's effective call of sinners through Jesus Christ is not based upon the assertion of individual rights. Such assertiveness, though characteristic of modern political equality, is destructive of the spiritual equality of all Christians. For self-assertion denies the grace of God in much the same way as the person who claims to be humble calls his humility in question in making the claim. Christian equality is characterised not by the mutual self-assertion of rights but by mutual submission.

THE CALL OF GOD AND FREEDOM

Sometimes the Bible expresses man's plight as imprisonment, as bondage. A person who is outside Christ is a willing captive, willing because he does not, left to himself, choose any other position. And yet his manner of life, when lived out consistently, is a denial of his humanity, for sin has a constricting and distorting effect upon its captives. But Christ is a liberator. He brings deliverance to the captives, the recovering of sight to the blind (*Luke 4:18*). He proclaims the acceptable year of the Lord, the year of Jubilee, when slaves are freed and debts are paid (*Luke 4:19*).

The idea that Christ is a liberator is nowadays often taken to mean that He advocated political liberation from Roman oppression and that He was primarily concerned with the political needs of the poor. It is also held that, by implication, the Christian Church ought to follow Christ and, where need be, engage in political revolution on behalf of the oppressed. But an examination of Christ's actions and His teaching as recorded in the Gospels shows that this is not so. Christ had compassion on cases of individual need. But far from encouraging revolt or disaffection Christ clearly distinguished between political and spiritual authority (*Matt. 22:21*). And on the famous occasion of Peter's confession of Christ's messiahship at Caesarea Philippi (*Matt. 16:16*), when Peter remonstrated with Christ on hearing Him foretell His own capture and death, Christ regarded this protest as nothing less than a Satanic temptation. It seems that Peter believed at this stage that Jesus was a political Messiah who had arrived to overthrow the Romans. But Christ rebuked him, and the other disciples. He invited them to follow Him in self-denial.

On another occasion, when Christ was invited to become a judge and to adjudicate in a dispute over an inheritance He refused to do so (*Luke 12:14*) and used the occasion to warn people against covetousness. And, faced with crucifixion, Christ rebuked Peter's attempt to defend Him by the use of physical force (*John 18:36*), insisting that His kingdom was not of this world, and had no use for swords or other weapons. Could anything be clearer than that Christ was not a political revolutionary or liberator and that political change had no place in the coming of the kingdom?

But did He not take up the cause of the poor? When the disciples of John the Baptist came to Jesus to ask whether or not He was the Messiah did not Christ point John to the signs of His Messiahship, to the fact that the blind received their sight and that the poor had the gospel preached to them? (*Matt. 11:5*). When Christ taught in the synagogue, did He not claim to be fulfilling Old Testament prophecy in that He was the one whom the Lord had anointed to preach good news to the poor? (*Luke 4:18*). Did not Christ bless the poor and pronounce woe on the rich? (*Matt. 5:3, Luke 6:24*).

To assume that 'the poor' in these passages are those who have no money is to misunderstand what Christ was teaching. When announcing His mission to the poor Christ quoted from Isaiah 61 which is concerned with the proclaiming of forgiveness to the humble, to the God-fearing, to those who are 'poor in spirit'. So the term 'poor' has a spiritual rather than an economic or political meaning. It refers to those who do not trust to financial prosperity or political programmes to deliver them, but who trust in the divine mercy.

Christ warns more than once of the danger of riches. But He does not give this warning because riches are politically unacceptable, or because riches are always ill-gotten, but because money almost invariably has the effect of taking the heart away from God (*Luke 12:15*) though even in such cases God's grace is able to do the seemingly impossible (*Matt. 19:26*).

Yet while 'liberation theology' is an obvious distortion of the New Testament good news it is equally mistaken to think of Christian freedom as freedom to do whatever one wants to do without restraint.

Freedom from certain restraints is often a blessing. Thus it is a blessing to be free from the coercing and persecuting action of the state. But we are not to conclude from this that the state has no responsibilities to its members, nor that individuals have no responsibilities to the state (*Rom. 13:1–7*)), nor that it is of no importance what people believe and how, if at all, they worship. It is rather that a politically enforced religion is a contradiction in terms. And while the freedom to worship in public is valuable this does not mean that anyone ought to be free to worship exactly as he pleases. No religion is likely to be tolerated – or ought to be tolerated – which involved, say, human sacrifice, or the removal of children from their parents, or the opening-up of the graves of the recently-buried. Freedom of worship is freedom sanctioned by law. And this applies to freedom in other personal matters and in economic and social life. It might plausibly be argued that, due to the selfishness of men and women, it is not so much the law which restrains liberty as the law which prevents anarchy and makes liberty possible.

A measure of personal liberty, freedom from arbitrary coercion by others, is normally an advantage to the Christian church. It permits the preaching of the gospel in public and allows the development of Christian talent (*1 Tim. 2:2*). Yet political freedom is not essential to the church, which has existed and even flourished under conditions of persecution.

So while it would be mistaken to think of Christian freedom as 'liberation theology' envisages it, it would be equally wrong to think of it as a freedom to do what a person wants to do without any restraint.

It is true that when a person is effectively called by God's grace he is freed from the coercing and enslaving effects of sin. But he is not his own master. God's call unites a person to Christ (*Eph. 2:5,6*). And as a Christian the one who is called now strives to serve Christ, 'whose service is perfect freedom'. The Christian experiences moral and spiritual freedom.

Yet to describe this as 'moral' and 'spiritual' freedom does not mean that it is secret and private and that it has no bearing on everyday life. On the contrary, as Christ's servant the Christian begins to live in a way which fulfils his true, truly human, nature. Christian conversion is restoration, re-creation (*Eph. 4.24*). While the idea of 'recreation' clearly implies the sharpest kind of discontinuity between the old life and the new life, what is being re-created is the true nature of men and women in God's knowledge and service.

To put it rather differently, the Christian is called to follow Christ, the last Adam, in whose image all who are in Him through faith share. They have His image partly now, completely hereafter (*Rom. 8:29*). And as Christ's character enabled Him to keep the law of God faultlessly, so the believer, being called to follow Christ, is called to keep God's law. So, paradoxically perhaps, Christian freedom consists in keeping the commandments of God. By his effective call by God's grace the believer is so changed – given a *new* nature – that he *wants* to keep God's law. As Paul puts it, he delights in the law of God after the inward man (*Rom. 7:22*). Before his conversion the law of God was a burden to him, a chain from which he wished to be free. Now his new nature, in conflict with the old, approves of the law of God. God's law is no longer thought of as a way in which God's favour might be gained, for Christ has gained forgiveness and righteousness for him by keeping the law of God and by dying as the suffering Saviour in his place. The law is now the rule of his life which he delights in and aims to uphold, an aim which brings continual clashes and conflicts between the 'old man' and the 'new man' (*Rom 7:22–24*).

Yet the Christian does not only have to keep the law of God. He has an actual, inspirational embodiment of such law-keeping in Christ. Jesus 'personalises' the law of God, not by adding to it or subtracting from it, but by summing it up and perfectly expressing it in His own life, in the drama of His earthly ministry and His self-offering on the cross. It is to Christ's example that the apostles frequently point (*Phil. 2:5*), as did Christ Himself (*John 13:3–17*) in order to inspire and to fire the moral imagination of believers.

[16]

Christ is not a mere moral teacher or hero. He whom the Christian is called to follow is the one who is his Saviour. Gratitude to God for such a Saviour provides the spur for Christian discipleship. Not the vain desire for self-salvation, or for a rigid and correct moralism, but the confident and well-grounded assurance that Christ has gained salvation for him moves the Christian to follow Christ.

So Christian freedom does not consist either in political liberation from poverty or oppression, or in the freedom to do whatever one wants to do, but in the *structured* freedom from the constraining power of sin to serve God in the keeping of His law. The Christian is not to use his freedom as an excuse for immorality but as an opportunity for service (*Gal. 5:13*).

To modern ears the word 'law' conjures up endless rules and regulations, sections and sub-sections, the detailed and complex legislation that is needed to govern a modern industrial society. But the Christian's relation to the law of Christ is not like, say, the relation of an employer to health and safety regulations. The Christian is not given a rule or regulation to cover every move he makes. Nor is he to want to have such a system of rules. Rather, the detailed application of the law of Christ in his own life must be worked out in the light of the application of the general principles of the law of God to his detailed circumstances. The Christian is called upon to exercise mature, and maturing, judgment. In similar circumstances to other Christians he may find himself differing as to what is the right thing for him to do, because, though similar, circumstances may nevertheless make important differences. The Christian may consult others in forming his conclusions about what to do. He may make use of accumulated Christian wisdom, or indeed anything else which he finds of help, but in the last resort the decision to follow Christ in *this* particular way is his, and his alone. This is another aspect of Christian freedom, the freedom to assess and judge situations for oneself. We shall take up these themes in more detail in chapter four.

AN EMERGING PATTERN

The call of God, the effective call which itself brings a response, does not come to one particular class or type of person, though often men and women who are otherwise insignificant are called by God's grace. Even so, God does not call and form His church on the basis of age or sex or race or income, but calls individuals from a wide variety of circumstances. Such people, in all their diversity and individuality, are called by grace into spiritual equality in the church. They are 'all one in Christ Jesus' (*Gal. 3:28*). This is one half of the pattern.

Yet the call of God to people of diverse backgrounds and types ought not to nullify or eliminate their individuality; rather it should elevate and transform it. This diversity covers not only the diversity of function within the church (*1 Cor. 12*) but also differences which are revealed in everyday life, differences which relate to work and leisure, and to family and cultural life. God's grace in Christ, although it ensures the equality and unity of all believers, does not reduce Christians to a lowest common denominator, ironing out all their individuality and making them into robots or zombies. Christians come from diverse backgrounds, and have widely differing talents and opportunities. But divine grace ought to elevate and transform the individuality of Christians. This is because the person who is effectively called by God's grace has the desire to serve God, moved by gratitude for what God has done for him through Christ. Such a person wants to follow every command of God.

[18]

Summing up, what we have seen can be expressed as follows: *the effective call of God, while it secures the spiritual equality and unity of those who are called, does not eliminate human diversity but transforms it.*

Does this mean that Christians adopt a distinctive 'life-style'? Yes and no. It depends partly upon their circumstances. The life of a person who is a Christian in a Hindu village in rural India will be very different from that of his Hindu neighbours, while that of a Christian in modern Europe will usually be less conspicuous. Great as any such contrasts may be, there can never be an absolute contrast, as if the Hindu and the Christian had nothing in common. Any society must have certain public standards of honesty, respect for property and for family life, and the obligation to meet certain essentials. Such matters are generally consistent with the law of God even though many other aspects of the manner of life of a Hindu – or the average city-dweller in Europe – will be distasteful to the Christian and may present acute personal difficulties for him.

The law of God which the Christian is called to obey is not alien to his true nature. It is that law which, when lived consistently, enables a person to be truly himself, not a member of a different species, but a full human being. And so it follows that the law expresses many values and meets many needs that someone who is not a Christian will at once recognise as being among *his* needs. Even those without the law often do the things contained in the law, as Paul says (*Rom. 2:14*). Some of these have already been mentioned – the need for honesty in dealings, for the maintenance of family life, for respect for human life and property – these are the most obvious, and they are observed in part the world over, simply because without them no society could exist. And so Christian freedom does not require that a person leaves society, to live alone in the desert or in a remote commune, though there may be some situations in which the Christian is forced to stand aloof, as well as many practices in which it would be inconsistent for him to engage.

So the distinctiveness of the Christian is not always to be found in what he does but in the motives which bind him to his Lord. For he strives to serve and emulate Christ, while the non-Christian lives in a way which ignores the claims of God on him, or even in a way which is hostile to such claims.

Yet sometimes the Christian *is* called upon to be different from others precisely because he is called to follow Christ. In his first letter Peter was faced with the problem of how Christian slaves were to behave, particularly when they had hostile and awkward masters who made them suffer. Peter begins by distinguishing between that suffering which is brought about by a person's own sinful failure and that which comes simply because the person in question is a Christian. A Christian ought not to suffer as an evil-doer. And yet it may be that a Christian will suffer simply because he is a Christian. For instance, in Peter's time the Christian who was a slave might have to refuse to do what he regarded as immoral and to run the risk of punishment. What ought he to do? Ought he to change his behaviour, or to run away? According to Peter the Christian slave was to draw inspiration from the example of Christ who neither looked for revenge nor became deceitful but who committed himself to the righteous judgment of God (*1 Pet. 2:21–3*).

Here was a clear occasion on which the non-Christian and the Christian slave might be expected to behave differently. For when a person suffers it is 'natural' for him to look for revenge. Peter advised against this, and counselled the Christian slave to be consistently Christian – and to behave accordingly. Peter even went so far as to say that Christians are 'called' to such a life (*1 Pet. 2:21*). To respond in this way to suffering was a part of God's appointment no matter when such an occasion might arise. Peter here introduces a further aspect of 'calling', which is different from though related to the effective call of God's grace. It is to this further aspect that attention is to be given in what follows.

2: *The Dangers of a Double Mind*

The men and women who are effectively called by God do not live in a cultural vacuum or in a world of their own. Everyone is partly the product of his or her social circumstances, and picks up innumerable beliefs and attitudes without thinking twice about them. And the people who become Christians are no exceptions to this general rule. Although God has ordered and 'bounded' their lives even before their conversion (as He orders and bounds the lives of all men) yet the pre-conversion lives of Christians are not noticeably different from the rest. Everyone takes it for granted that the earth goes round the sun, that the blood circulates and that bread nourishes. Such beliefs mould further beliefs and behaviour, in the Christian as well as in everyone else.

For while God's call by grace is supernatural, unmerited and unaccountable in terms of genes and upbringing, yet God calls people who are by this time influenced and shaped by the world around them, with personalities which are already formed or at least (in the case of children) partly-formed. And while regenerating grace exerts a deep influence upon people – they are 'new creatures in Christ' (*2 Cor. 5:17*) – such grace does not make them completely different people. A conversion is not like radical brain-surgery. John Smith, when he is converted, is still John Smith. He does not literally become another person, nor is he transported to some earthly paradise, or to a community of angels or to heaven itself. He continues to live at the old address, he works at the same office or factory and he has the same relations and acquaintances. He suffers from the same aches and pains and from the same peculiarities of character. He leads one life. Conversion does not erase all his memories as a motor-bike accident might do, nor does it produce hallucinations in the way that LSD does. Paradoxically, although he changes, he still remains the same.

All this is commonplace. Yet one of the most powerful influences on Christians and the Christian church over the centuries has been a tendency to think about human living in such a way as to *divide up* its reality in a radical but mistaken way. So powerful are these influences upon Christian attitudes that they may create a strong undertow of which most are scarcely aware. Such a claim may seem to be both strange and extreme but when we shortly consider certain instances of it, recognition will be easy. Such thinking – let us call it *dualistic thinking* – has been a recurring problem throughout the history of the Christian church, taking different forms at different times.

But what is dualism and what is 'dualistic thinking'? The basic idea behind all dualistic attitudes is that all reality (or an important part of it) is thought to be made up of sets of forces or attitudes which are in irreconcilable opposition to one another. One very influential dualistic idea, for example, is that the universe is divided into two 'realities', physical reality and spiritual reality. And these two realities are supposedly opposed to each other, like an acid and an alkali. If a person is not to be torn apart in the battle between them then he is forced to choose one or the other. This will be explained more fully shortly.

Quite distinct from such dualistic thinking, and not to be confused with it, is the *tension* that a person may feel in his life. A person may feel a tension between the pleasures or needs of the present and those of the future. He may want to stay in bed but he has to get up for work. Some may live wholly for the present, or wholly for the future. Alternatively a person may feel a tension between his own individual needs and responsibilities and those of a wider community, his family or church or nation.

The New Testament itself stresses the tension between 'this world' and 'the world to come'. It is a truism that we all live in this world, in the present. But Christians are also faced with the claims and the prospective joys of 'the world to come'. The Christian feels this tension, the pull of both worlds, between present responsibilities and future glory.

Such tension is inevitable, even healthy, whether it is the tension between the present and the future in this life, or the peculiarly Christian tension between this world and that to come. The Apostle Paul clearly felt this (*Phil. 1:23,24*). But while *tension* of this sort is acceptable, the dualistic frame of mind which would actively *oppose* one aspect of reality to another is unacceptable and dangerous.

The difference between *tension* and *opposition* may seem to be small and trivial. Nevertheless it is of the first importance. For while the Christian feels the tension between this world and the world to come, it is a mistake to think that there is a fundamental opposition between this world and the world to come and that the Christian ought to make a choice between them. A Christian is not a person for whom all that matters is heaven and who has no need to eat and sleep and keep himself clean. It is equally wrong to think that all that matters is this present moment to the total exclusion of the future. While there is tension, nowhere in the New Testament is it suggested that there is a basic opposition or incompatibility between the two, nor is the Christian invited to choose one at the expense of the other. So there is tension but not opposition, and because there is no opposition there should be no dualism in our thinking.

DUALISM AND THE CALL OF GOD

Recognising this fundamental difference between tension and opposition, we must next ask why dualistic thinking is so dangerous for the Christian. The danger is that the Christian, without actively thinking about the matter, but by unconsciously absorbing ideas from outside, will come to understand the call of God in a dualistic fashion. He may understand his conversion as involving the severing of all ties with the present world, the minimising of contacts and responsibilities with it, in order to concentrate his attention wholly upon the world to come.

This may seem to some to be far-fetched. But several of the warnings of the apostolic writings appear to be aimed at heading off such an attitude. It seems that the early Thessalonian church, or some members of it, were strongly inclined not to engage in daily work but to live in idle expectation of the Second Coming of Christ. Paul's advice to the slaves at Corinth (to be examined in greater detail in the next chapter) seems intended to oppose the idea that when a person is related to Christ no other relationships matter but may be broken at will (*1 Cor. 7:20*). And John's reminder to the churches that Jesus Christ has come in the flesh (*1 John 1:1*) appears designed to counteract the idea that Christianity is a purely 'spiritual' religion in which the human body has no essential place (*1 John 4:2,3*). Dualisms of various kinds were waiting in the wings at the time of the early church and from time to time since have occupied centre-stage.

It is clear that the New Testament contrast between 'two worlds' is not to be taken literally. The Christian is not called to leave the physical world for some spiritual world, or to suppose that physical matter is evil and that therefore the Incarnation did not really occur.

Sometimes the pull of dualism may be felt in another area. The New Testament teaches that before his conversion a person is living a life of unreality. He has false beliefs about himself and the world around him, and at his conversion he 'comes to himself' (*Luke 15:17*), recognising the plain truth of his relationship to God. He regains, or begins to regain, his true nature as a person made in God's image and his place in God's revealed purpose for mankind (*1 Cor. 15:22*). What more natural, given such teaching, than for a person to think that now that he has become a Christian and has come face to face with reality he must, in the name of Christ, attempt to redeem society. And so some Christians come to identify their calling as Christians almost wholly in 'this worldly' terms – in fostering the economic development of the Third World, in pressing for reform in housing or prisons, in the preservation of the physical environment, or in some other similar cause. The concern of other Christians with their personal standing before God, and their own concern with such matters, is dismissed as 'pietism' and 'escapism'.

One theme of this book is that the pull of one or other of the supposed polar opposites of such dualisms ought to be resisted by the Christian. The only biblical 'dualism' is that between righteousness and sin. The New Testament provides good grounds for thinking that any other dualistic thinking – and we shall shortly consider various examples, with exclusive emphasis being placed on one side of the dualism or the other – is not characteristically Christian but is positively unChristian. In order to show that the emphasis upon the dangers of dualism is not an exaggerated one, and also to focus our thoughts more clearly on the character of such dualistic thinking, a brief glance will be taken at three different eras of Christian history to show dualism's recurring influence.

THREE CASE STUDIES

(i) *Augustine and evil.* In the thought-world of the time immediately after the Apostles one of the most potent intellectual influences at the margins of the Christian church was Manicheism. Few of the actual writings of Mani have survived, although the contents of several of them can be surmised and to some extent reconstructed from the references to them in the extant writings of those who attempted to refute Manicheism.

Mani (AD 216–c.276) was a Persian who taught, as a result of having received certain 'revelations', that there are two eternal principles, God (or light) and matter, and these two principles are in everlasting conflict. Each human being is an instance of light being entrapped in matter (the soul or spirit embodied in physical flesh) and redemption is to be effected by ascetic abstinence. Following the return of Jesus the elect are to be reunited with light at the destruction of the material creation.

Such a teaching, summarised in this fashion, involving a dualism of matter (inherently evil) and spirit (inherently good), may seem bizarre and far-fetched. Yet it was enormously influential in the ancient world, and its attractions are still being felt wherever there is teaching to the effect that the body is inherently evil. A version of this dualism is also expressed when people say that the universe is the battlefield between two equal forces, God and the Devil.

Something of the power and fascination that Manicheism exerted even over highly intelligent people can be seen from studying the life of Augustine of Hippo

(354–430). For about nine years before his conversion Augustine was attracted by Manicheism and greatly influenced by its dualistic teaching. According to his own account he

> believed that evil, too, was some similar kind of substance, a shapeless, hideous mass, which might be solid, in which case the Manichees call it earth, or fine and rarefied like air. This they imagine as a kind of evil mind filtering through the substance they call earth. And because such little piety as I had compelled me to believe that God, who is good, could not have created an evil nature, I imagined that there were two antagonistic masses, both of which were infinite, yet the evil in a lesser and the good in a greater degree.

Augustine recounts in his *Confessions* that one of the great obstacles to his becoming a Christian was the Manichean teaching about evil. For the idea of an eternal conflict between God and evil suggested to him that God was corruptible, and so that he could be overcome, and this is clearly inconsistent with biblical teaching. And yet the reality of evil cannot be denied. It is certainly not a phantom or a trick of the imagination. Augustine was drawn to look for a solution to the problem of the nature of evil in astrology, but without success. Eventually he came to believe that evil is not an eternal principle but that it is a deficiency, a want, just as hunger and blindness are wants or deficiencies, and that such a deficiency was permitted by an all-powerful and an all-good God. He realised that evil was due not simply to the will of men but more particularly and basically to the permission of God. He reflected upon the issue as follows:

> Where then does evil come from, if God made all things and, because He is good, made them good too? It is true that He is the supreme Good, that He is Himself a

greater Good than these lesser goods which He created. But the Creator and all His creation are both good. Where then does evil come from? Can it be that there was something evil in the matter from which He made the universe? When He shaped this matter and fitted it to His purpose, did He leave in it some part which He did not convert to good? But why should He have done this? Are we to believe that, although He is omnipotent, He had not the power to convert the whole of this matter to good and change it so that no evil remained in it? Why, indeed, did He will to make anything of it at all?

And Augustine came finally to realise that

When I asked myself what wickedness was, I saw that it was not a substance but perversion of the will when it turns aside from you, O God, who are the supreme substance, and veers towards things of the lowest order.

What Augustine came to see was that evil is not matter, neither is it linked to matter, but it is due to the perversion of a created will, a perversion permitted by the all-good God. Evil is not an eternal principle but the absence of a principle, lawlessness, giving rise to enmity and rebellion.

Although Augustine's understanding of evil as a privation or deficiency was of deep importance for the history of Christian thought, what is of more significance here is the influence upon him, for a time, of the matter-spirit dualism. For although the thought-world of Augustine is sharply different from our own, patterns of thinking have the habit of remaining remarkably stable.

(ii) *Anabaptism*. In the case of Augustine and the Manichean view of evil the dualism between matter (darkness, evil) and spirit (light, goodness) is rather abstract and, though influential, it is difficult to grasp and to state clearly. But the thought of the church has also been affected by dualistic thinking about more concrete matters, such as society and its organisation.

Each of us grows up in a world of 'societies' – families, clubs, schools, firms and the like. Some Christian societies have been so impressed with the fact that being a Christian involved being a member of a new society – the church – that they have been strongly tempted to break all other ties that have existed between the Christian and human societies or at least to reduce the area of contact to an absolute minimum. They have held that a Christian is to be a member of only one society. Or, if there are to be other societies they are to be related to the church, under whose wing all other activities take place, in an arrangement that might accurately be called an ecclesiocracy, government by the church. It is difficult to find a case in history where all such ties have been totally severed, a case of total exclusivism, because it is almost impossible to achieve such a position. Nevertheless repeated attempts have been made to form 'separate' groups whose connections with the rest of society are minimal, and from time to time attempts have been made to carry out such plans with great thoroughness and determination.

Such an attempt was made during the mediaeval period. One of the aims of the monastic movement was to free itself from the contaminating influences of the surrounding society. The movement consisted of 'communities specially endowed and set apart for the full, lifelong, and irrevocable practice of the Christian life at a level of excellence judged to be impossible outside such a community' (R. W. Southern). It is not often realised how widespread such communities were. Southern estimates that there were at one period over eight hundred monastries in England and Wales alone. Such an attempt at Christian excellence by separation was doomed to failure, because it failed to reckon with the fact that the most potent source of contamination is a person's own heart and mind. Nor surprisingly, therefore, Southern says that anyone who looks at such communities for a pure expression of the aims of their founders must very often be disappointed. Wherever the human heart and mind go, evil is sure to go as well. And in abandoning family life as the norm monasticism was productive of much additional evil.

Such influences certainly reappeared during the upheavals of the Reformation. At that time various Anabaptist groups formed on the continent of Europe (and to a lesser extent among the Separatists of the Elizabethan period in England), and then at a later period in North America where they were often driven by persecution. In intention these were self-governing, communistic communities (appealing to Acts 2:44) withdrawn from the society around them, and particularly from the corrupt church. Society was corrupt and corrupting, under the sway of Satan, and so the natural thing to do was to establish independent groupings which, it was held, foreshadowed and were to await the millennial reign of Christ. Accordingly it was characteristic of Anabaptism that its adherents refused political office and responsibility – to serve as magistrates, to pay taxes – as a matter of principle. As one of their Confessions of Faith expresses it

> It is not appropriate for a Christian to serve as a magistrate because of these points: The government magistracy is according to the flesh, but the Christians' is according to the Spirit; their houses and dwelling remain in this world, but the Christians' are in heaven; their citizenship is in this world, but the Christians' citizenship is in heaven; the weapons of their conflict and war are carnal and against the flesh only, but the Christians' weapons are spiritual, against the fortification of the devil.

[31]

Naturally enough such groups aroused the hostility of governments because they were perceived to be a political threat, and there was a great deal of persecution. But what is of concern here is not the historical fate of the Anabaptist movement but the sort of thinking which gave rise to it and to movements and tendencies like it. In coming to understand such thinking we are driven to the conclusion that such groups saw not simply a *contrast* between society at large and the society of the church, a contrast which gives rise to tension, as the New Testament indicates in many places (*Heb. 13:14, Phil. 3:20*), but they saw an immediate and unrelieved *opposition* between the two, a dualism between the old society, 'the world', and the new society, 'the church'.

(iii) *Faith and History*. Not all cases of dualistic thinking are as ancient as those we have looked at so far. One 'new' dualism, one that is characteristic of some forms of modern theological thinking, is that which alleges the existence of a radical difference between the Christian faith on the one hand and the facts of history on the other.

It is fundamental to Christianity that certain publicly-witnessed historical events took place. Without these events there could be no good news, for the gospel is the good news of what God has done in the person of His Son incarnate. In this sense history is the vehicle of our redemption. 'Jesus Christ was born of the virgin Mary, suffered under Pontius Pilate, was crucified, dead and buried . . .' Such was the confession of the church in the post-Apostolic period, the Middle Ages, the time of the Reformation, and virtually until the eighteenth century. Then there arose a way of thinking, mainly on the continent of Europe, but later also in Scotland and England, which attempted to separate matters of Christian 'faith' from the events of human 'history'. And not only to separate them, but in some cases to set them in opposition. One argument for this separation, made famous by the German thinker Lessing (1729–81), emphasised the view that matters of history were uncertain, the subject of conjecture and endless debate. How then could the 'certainties' of the Christian faith be based upon, or require, the vagaries of historical research and its findings? Another argument, advanced by the German philosopher Immanuel Kant (1724–1804), claimed that on philosophical grounds the knowledge of God is impossible because God is beyond any possible human experience. Christian faith could not therefore be based upon what God has been pleased to bring about in the history of human affairs, His self-revelation in Christ. God, said Kant, cannot reveal Himself. There cannot be knowledge of God. Rather, true Christian faith ('pure religious faith' as Kant called it) is divorced from any supposed knowledge of God and is based upon morality. This 'pure faith' is to be sharply contrasted with the various 'ecclesiastical faiths' which depend upon an acceptance of the authority of Scripture and, through Scripture, upon what happened in history. Kant expressed his outlook in this way:

> The final purpose even of reading these holy scriptures, or of investigating their content, is to make men better; the historical element, which contributes nothing to this end, is something which is in itself quite indifferent, and we can do with it what we like.

Kant's view is that the Christian faith has only to do with the teaching of certain moral ideals, and with motivating people to act morally, and that faith does not depend upon the knowledge of God or of what He has been pleased to do in human history. This view has been extremely influential in Protestant theology since the eighteenth century. According to Kant, whether Christ's resurrection really occurred, is an interesting speculative matter but of no concern to true faith, which can – and must – function perfectly well whatever the historical facts turn out to be. For faith is not a matter of trusting God as He has revealed Himself in the Incarnate and written word, but of sincere adherence to certain moral principles.

What Lessing and Kant (and the scores of theologians who have followed them in this) are saying is not that there are tensions or difficulties in the area of faith and historical enquiry, but that there is a fundamental opposition between the two, a dualism of faith and history. So, they say, Christian faith has nothing to do with the facts and theories of history nor, if it is to retain its character as 'pure faith', can it be linked with history.

One practical effect of this dualism between faith and history (and a similar dualism between faith and natural science) has been to make the Christian religion, in the eyes of some, a wholly private affair, a matter of personal feeling or attitude or motive, having no point of contact with the public world of fact. Another, opposite practical effect, has been to make Christianity a wholly public affair, having to do solely with social and political change, and even with revolution. For in some versions of the dualism between faith and history, Christian faith has wholly to do with social morality, with changing the world for the better. Every Christian knows what it is like to feel a tension between faith and history, and between his public and his private life. It has been the achievement of much modern Protestant theology to change that familiar tension into outright opposition, into a dualism according to which faith cannot have any stake in history. Perhaps this is the old Manichean dualism in yet another of its guises.

DUALISM AND THE NEW TESTAMENT

The reason for sketching the three case studies is to illustrate how persistent dualistic thinking has been in the history of the Christian church, and to show how easy it is to set some features of God's created reality in opposition to other features, matter to spirit, or history to faith. As a result the life of the Christian has been set forth not as one integrated life, with recognisable tensions, but as a two-level life in which (in the examples considered) physical matter, or human society, or human history have come to be regarded as wholly alien to true Christian faith.

But some may say that the contention that the Christian should resist such dualistic thinking is made too hastily. For it might be claimed that some of this so-called dualistic thinking is to be found in the teaching of the New Testament itself. If so it is not so much a dangerous departure from the Christian faith as characteristic of and even essential to true Christian thinking. For when Paul contrasts 'flesh' and 'spirit' (*Gal. 5:17*), and when John warns against 'the world', are they not being dualistic? In order to see whether or not this is so we must glance briefly at what they say.

(i) *'Flesh and 'Spirit'*. The contrast between 'flesh' and 'spirit' is drawn by Paul throughout his writings, particularly in Romans 7, Galatians 5 and 1 Corinthians 15. He says that in the Christian flesh and spirit are in irreconcilable conflict, that flesh and blood cannot inherit the kingdom of God, that those who live after the flesh mind the things of the flesh, and so on. One of the meanings of 'flesh' is 'meat' and it is easy to suppose that by 'flesh' Paul means 'physical body'. One of the meanings of 'spirit' is 'soul' and so it is easy to suppose that by 'spirit' Paul means 'soul'. And so, it is argued, when Paul talks about a conflict between flesh and spirit, he is drawing a contrast between 'body' and 'soul' and in effect saying that the Christian will experience a conflict between his body and his soul as long as he lives, and that there will be no place for bodies in the kingdom of God.

Such an understanding of what Paul is saying is attractive because the conflict between the mind and the body is commonplace. It is something that each of us experiences at first hand. Who has not known what it is to want to do something – to enjoy a book, or see the sights of a city, or talk to a friend – and yet to be prevented from doing so by tiredness or sickness? Or of having to fulfil an obligation but being too lazy to do it? And what is more striking than the contrast between the human mind, with its capacity for thinking in abstract and ideal ways, and the human body, with its limitations imposed by feebleness, disease and inevitable decay? Are these not cases of the flesh being in conflict with the spirit, the conflict of which Paul writes in Romans 7?

No, they are not. There are occasions when Paul uses 'flesh' literally, meaning 'body', and times when he uses the term figuratively or metaphorically, and these uses must not be confused. When it is used literally the term 'flesh' means either the body, the whole of physical existence (*Gal. 1:16*) or physical descent (*Rom. 9:5*) or even to the body as weakened through the effect of sin (*Rom. 8:36*). But when Paul uses the term figuratively it refers, not to the human body as distinct from the soul or spirit, but to the whole of the life of the non-Christian man as that life is lived in neglect of God or in opposition to God. A 'fleshly' man in this sense is not necessarily a sensual person. He may be an aesthete, an intellectual, or an ascetic. Nevertheless if he lives such a life in opposition to God he is, according to Paul, living 'in the flesh', and 'minding' the things of the flesh.

[36]

In a parallel way 'spirit' is sometimes used by Paul to refer to a person's inner character, his consciousness and self-awareness, the sum total of his mental powers, his mind (*I Cor. 2:11*). But where Paul uses it in contrast to the 'flesh' it signifies the human personality regarded as renewed and sanctified by the Holy Spirit (*Rom. 8:6*). The contrast between 'flesh' and 'spirit' in Paul is thus not a metaphysical contrast, a contrast between different kinds of substances, but an ethical and spiritual contrast, between two different ways in which human life is organised and directed. It is the contrast between the 'old man', life lived apart from God, and the 'new man', the new nature, God-loving and God-serving, a new nature which is imparted to the individual by God the Holy Spirit in the effectual call by grace.

This important distinction, accurately drawn, reinforces what was stressed earlier, that the Bible never characterises conversion, the effectual call, as a movement out of the body, but rather as a divinely-empowered turning of the whole man, a human person in his sensory, intellectual and moral aspects, to God. Such a person, being converted, is 'in the Spirit'; he no longer 'serves the flesh' even though the 'old man', his unregenerate nature, remains to haunt and trouble him, humbling him and keeping him dependent upon God for fresh grace.

According to Paul, therefore, the 'spiritual life' is not the life of the mind as distinct from the life of the body. Naturally enough there are times in a Christian's life when the mind is chiefly engaged, and when the body is relatively restful. Prayer, study, debate, meditation and self-examination, are such times. But even here, of course, the body is functioning, because a person does not leave his body to study the Bible or to pray. Tiredness, slothfulness and illness may all prevent or hinder such activities. And yet to suppose that the 'spiritual life' *consists in* such activities is to be guilty of a simple confusion. It is essential for us to eat and drink, and yet human life does not consist in eating and drinking.

And so the 'spiritual life' or the 'Christian life' is the whole of a person's life insofar as it is lived in accordance with the revealed will of God and prompted and empowered for this by the Holy Spirit. The development of the senses, in the appreciation of colour and sound, or in the employment of bodily skills, in gardening or engineering or painting, can be equally a part of the 'Christian life' as the more intellectual and devotional aspects of life. More to the point, devotion may properly express itself in the appropriate use of these skills for God's glory.

(ii) *'The world'*. This conclusion about the nature of the Christian life can be reinforced by remembering that the universe that each person lives in is God's universe. In the same way that the human body and the senses are not objectionable as such, and therefore not to be shunned or neglected, so the world of sights and sounds and practical opportunities is God's world.

But here, as with the discussion of 'flesh' earlier, care is needed in order to gain a proper appreciation of the biblical teaching. It is customary for us, in everyday speech, often to use the words 'earth' and 'world' as roughly equivalent. If someone talks about 'the world around us' he is probably drawing our attention to some aspect of the physical environment, perhaps to the vanishing rain forests or the life-style of the bat. But sometimes we may talk about a 'worldly' person, or about 'the world' getting on top of us, and here our usage comes closer to the distinctively biblical teaching about 'the world'.

It is certainly clear that when some of the biblical writers, notably John and Paul, use the word 'world' they use it not to refer to the earth, the planet with all its physical powers

[38]

and properties, but to some aspect, or aspects, of unbelieving man's alienation from God. The 'world' which Christ came to save (*John 3:16*) was not the earth, but creation in its sin, and John is emphasising in that verse the depth and the intensity of the divine love. God's love was so great as to love *the world*, those who are organised in opposition to him, and who use the creation to oppose its Creator. For such the Saviour was sent.

And so, once again, the contrast between 'world' and 'world' is not between two worlds, like two Chinese boxes, any more than the contrast between 'flesh' and 'flesh' is between two different kinds of body. It is a contrast not of stuff or substance but of motivation and end. A worldly man is a man who uses the beneficial gifts of God for the wrong end and with the wrong motive. The Christian is effectively called by grace, but is nevertheless still a mixture of motives, some worldly, some godly. Hence the conflict, which is another way of expressing the enmity between flesh and spirit.

When a person is called by grace, although he has a new nature, and is for that reason no longer 'of the world' (*1 Cor. 2:12*) yet he is still in the world. He is 'in the world' in the sense that there is a strong aspect of his nature which is still worldly, and in the world in the further sense that he lives and mixes with people who are not Christian. Indeed Paul emphasises the absurdity of supposing that a Christian might go out of the world (*1 Cor. 5:10*). He must of necessity rub shoulders with those who are not called by divine grace.

Although some jobs and 'life-styles' are more worthwhile than others, according to the New Testament there are no jobs which are worthwhile which take a person out of the world, nor should the attempt be made to find them. For not only does a person take his old nature with him wherever he goes, he also meets 'the world' wherever he meets and works with other people. This does not mean that the Christian should not aim to be distinctively Christian in all that he does. There are careers and courses of action which are intrinsically sinful, and situations in which a person may be brought under severe temptation to sin. It is obvious that these ought to be avoided. But this having been said, it is striking that the New Testament does not lay down any rules and regulations about what sort of employment is worthwhile for the Christian and what is not. And yet the reason for this is obvious. Cultural situations differ greatly from country to country and from time to time, as do people's aptitudes and skills. The New Testament does not provide an endless list of do's and don'ts, a directory of employment opportunities for Christians. Instead, as befits those who are called to maturity as adults in Christ (*Eph. 4:13–15*), it provides believers with principles and with promises of wisdom and guidance to apply these principles to the endlessly varied circumstances of human life.

So there is nothing about the nature of the Christian faith, either in its content or in how it is to be presented and received, to suggest that working and living a life in the world is inconsistent for the Christian, or unworthy of the gospel, or spiritually second-rate. Instead the New Testament emphasises that the believer, being effectively called by divine grace, is made in God's image. He is in God's world, and he has a mandate to subdue the creation for the greater glory of the Creator. The gospel provides a new appetite and vitality and a new sense of direction to serve God in this way.

And so the support that the New Testament may seem to give for the various kinds of dualism that we have been considering in this chapter is only apparent. The plain fact is that Scripture teaches two important truths which, when fully appreciated, will deliver believers for ever from any such dualism.

In the first place God's creation is good, and good in itself. It is not a Vanity Fair from which people must flee, nor a shadowy and unreal world behind which lies a spiritual world of real value. It is God's creation and it is good in all its aspects. No greater tribute to this fact could be provided than that the New Testament portrays the redemption of the church as a new creation (*2 Cor. 5:17*) and that God uses aspects of his creation to describe himself and to make himself intelligible and comprehensible to us (*Luke 1:76*). The only general limitation that Scripture places upon the present creation lies in the warning that in its present form it is not eternal, but fading and perishing, and that the Christian is not to strive for permanency in what is impermanent, but instead to look for that city which has foundations, whose Builder and Maker is God (*Heb. 11:10*). Perversion in the creation has arisen not from the creation itself but from the fact of sin and the curse of God upon sin. Rebellion against God has resulted in the abuse and distortion of the powers and agencies of the creation. But it is wrong to argue from this abuse of the creation that the created order is itself bad or harmful and that all must try to hide away from it. Scripture nowhere teaches this.

In the second place Scripture emphasises the sovereignty of God over the visible and invisible creation. As Job learned (*Job 42:1–6*) and as Scripture uniformly teaches (*Eph. 1:11, Isaiah 45:7*), the universe is not the theatre of war between two principles locked in eternal conflict. God the Lord is sovereign. Evil and sin occur by His permission, and not as the result of His failure or weakness or ignorance. It is by His will, for purposes and ends whose dim outline is revealed to us but whose detail is locked away (*John 13:7*), that sin and evil occur (*Amos*

3:6). It is by His righteous will (*Acts 2:23*) and for His glory (*Rom. 11:36*) that all things, including sin and evil, come to pass. And the Lord does not have to give an account of His doings to anyone, least of all to us (*Rom. 9:20,21*).

If we wish to retain dualistic language at all (and some of the dangers of such language have been noted) then the only 'dualism' that the Bible countenances is that between righteousness and sin. These are the great incompatibles. But sin, as Augustine saw so vividly, is not located in an eternal cosmic principle, but in the perverted human will.

These two great biblical assertions, the goodness of the creation and God's Lordship over it, are brought together in *divine providence*. God's supremacy over His creation is not like that of an absentee landlord. He is not detached or aloof but He is concerned with every last detail of what occurs. God is transcendent, above and beyond His creation (*Genesis 1:1*) and yet He sustains it and works in it, so much so that there is a sense in which the creation is 'in' God (*Acts 17:28*). It is therefore absurd to suppose that God is concerned with 'faith' or 'religion' or 'souls' but not with the grand sweep of history or of the innumerable individual actions which make it up. History is simply the unfolding of His purpose in space and time as far as this purpose concerns human affairs. The business of kings is in His hands (*Prov. 21:1*), as is the fall of a sparrow (*Matt. 10:29*). Days of evil and adversity (*Job 2:10*) as well as prosperity and blessing (*Matt. 5:45*) are under His sovereign control. His providential purposes had as one end the 'fulness of time' (*Gal. 4:4*) when Christ came and was offered up in accordance with His will (*John 9:4*), the lamb slain from the foundation of the world (*Rev. 13:8*), and when salvation was preached at the command of the Son of God (*Matt. 28:19*). And God's providence still brings all to pass, secretly and mysteriously, that it might serve the purposes of His kingdom, the consummation of all things in Christ (*Col. 1:19*), to the praise of the glory of His grace (*Eph. 1:6*).

Such an account is far from being dualistic. And yet there is no denying the fact that bouts of dualistic thinking periodically affect the church, and such thinking always seems to be bubbling away beneath the surface. This reminds us that 'living the Christian life' is not a romantic or sentimental affair, but that it calls for the reintegration of a life that has been split apart by sin. But how can these unwelcome, dualistic influences be reduced to a minimum? An attempt will now be made to try to answer this question by taking up again the theme of the divine calling which was sketched in the first chapter and in extending this, as the Bible itself does, beyond conversion – effectual calling – to include the whole of the Christian's life.

3: *Having a Calling*

The discussion of the last chapter was a reminder of one simple and yet basic fact. The Christian lives *one life*. Split-mindedness between *spiritual* and *secular*, or between *faith* and *history* is foreign to the New Testament and ought to be foreign to Christian experience. Bearing this basic fact in mind it is now possible to consider further the idea of the Christian's calling.

The effectual call of God which brings a person to new life in Christ is a historical event, taking place in a particular set of circumstances. The conversion itself may not be a datable occurrence, though for some, for instance Paul and Augustine, it certainly was. But whether a person's conversion to Christ is sudden or gradual, conversion takes place in life. As if to emphasise this, the New Testament frequently indicates something of this personal, everyday distinctiveness. Matthew was a tax-collector, Lydia a seller of purple cloth, Zacchaeus was a rich man, Cornelius a centurion, and so on.

Not only does the converting call of God come to people who are occupied with the business of life, those who are effectually called by God are normally called to remain in that life. The comparatively few exceptions to this ought not to detract from the basic pattern. An attempt will be made in this chapter and the next to develop its implications.

What are the exceptions? In the days of the New Testament some were personally called by Christ to form the inner group of His followers, the twelve apostles. Each of these, at the call of Christ, left what he was doing and followed Christ 'full time' (*Matt. 4:19,20*). Such an event was exceptional and there is no reason to expect from the teaching of the remainder of Scripture, and particularly from the instructions of the apostles themselves, that such cases form the norm or pattern for Christian discipleship.

Others recorded in the New Testament were involved in a course of life which was clearly immoral when God's call came to them. The freedom which comes as a result of God's effectual call is, as was seen in chapter one, the freedom willingly to follow the law of God based upon a delight in its righteousness. If so, then any one who is converted when he is leading a life of crime or debauchery, or who has an occupation the very nature of which is unlawful, is required by the gospel to leave it. This applies to a false religion as well as to an immoral way of life.

Many to whom Paul wrote in the church at Corinth had been extortioners. They had gained money through false-pretences, or by making Mafia-style threats, or through charging crippling rates of interest. In writing to them Paul reminds them of their past life and of the fact that they had now been 'washed' (*1 Cor. 6:11*). Their style of life and the way in which they gained their living had been changed. Paul wrote to the Ephesians that those who stole were to steal no more but to engage in lawful work, work that was in accordance with the law of God and therefore in accordance with the manner of life to which, as Christians, they had been called (*Eph. 4:28*).

Allowing for such exceptions it is absolutely clear from the pattern of teaching in the New Testament that people who are effectually called by God's grace are to fulfil their callings by remaining where they are.

THE TWO CALLINGS AGAIN

Paul's first letter to the Corinthians was written to a church with many complex problems. Among these was a misunderstanding which had arisen about Christian conversion and its effect upon social and family life. For some of the Corinthian believers were developing an attitude which was ascetic. They so stressed their union with Christ that in their view it took the place of all other social ties and duties, including marriage. Some of the new Christians were so impressed by their call by grace, and by the difference that it had made to their lives, that they were tempted to sever the family and social ties to which they were already committed.

For instance, it happened that in the case of some married couples, one was converted and the other was not. What were they to do? Ought they to separate? Paul tells them that if the one who is not converted is content to maintain the marriage then the couple ought not to separate. If, on the other hand, the person who is unconverted separates from his or her partner, then Paul says that such separation is permissible for the Christian partner. But as far as possible – this is Paul's teaching – the relationship ought to be maintained both for its own sake, for it may result in the conversion of the unconverted partner, and for the sake of any children (*1 Cor. 7:14, 16*).

Paul is even more emphatic over the question of the responsibilities of Christians who were slaves at the time when they were converted. It seems that the Christian slaves were strongly tempted to stress the liberty that they now enjoyed in Christ and to flee from their masters. For was not their relationship to Christ the only one that mattered? But Paul warns against this. In fact he claims that an appreciation of their relationship to Christ should lead them to stay where they are (*1 Cor. 7:22*). The

Christian slave might think that his fellow-Christian who was not a slave was more free than he. Not so, says Paul. The Christian who is not a slave is the slave of Christ. And the Christian who is a slave to an earthly master is the Lord's freeman. As Paul says elsewhere, no Christian lives or dies to himself. For whether we live or die we are the Lord's (*Rom. 14:8*).

But it is also clear that Paul is not teaching the slaves to be fatalistic. It was characteristic of some Victorian, not to say mediaeval, attitudes to hold that each person had his place from childhood unchangeably fixed by God.

> The rich man in his castle,
> The poor man at his gate,
> He made them high and lowly,
> And ordered their estate.

But this is not Paul's teaching. He is not saying that a Christian who is newly converted should never change his situation. This is clear from verse 21, 'if thou mayest be made free, use it rather'. Paul teaches that there is a vast difference between using Christianity as an excuse to overturn established patterns of living, and being presented with an opportunity to change. If the opportunity comes it may be used. But if it does not come, then the Christian is not to think that he cannot be Christ's disciple where he is.

Paul's positive teaching is summed-up in the words 'Let every man abide in the same calling wherein he was called' (*v. 20*). His choice of words and what they imply are most interesting. They are of fundamental importance for an understanding of the Christian's relationship to daily life.

For Paul, a Christian is called while he is in a calling. That is, a person is effectually called by divine grace while he is in a particular situation in life and this situation (with the exceptions already noted) the Christian is to regard as a *calling*. It is the situation to which the Lord has 'assigned' him (NIV). Paul says that someone who is newly converted ought not immediately to look for a new situation, a new set of circumstances in which to live, but he ought to live as a Christian in the very same set of circumstances in which he finds himself. If anything, Paul's teaching is even stronger than this. The person is to *abide* in that calling, provided that the calling is a lawful one and that no legitimate opportunity arises for him to move out of it should he wish to do so.

So a Christian has two callings. He is effectually called by grace, converted. In addition there is a call of a different kind, that which is provided by the network of circumstance, personal relations, past history, in which he is found when God's grace comes to him.

It has been argued by such writers as Max Weber and R. H. Tawney that Protestantism, and more specifically Calvinism, created the conditions for the emergence of modern industrial capitalism partly through the Protestant emphases upon the worthwhileness of a 'secular' calling, on individual responsibility and on the growth of personal freedom. Whatever elements of truth may be in this argument Paul's idea of 'calling' is wider than the idea of daily work, though it includes it. It takes in not only work but every lawful link and relationship in a person's life.

What Paul's word 'calling' or 'assignment' implies is that this network of circumstances is not a person's 'lot' or 'fate'. Much less is it something a person should take refuge from by creating a purely 'spiritual' haven. Rather it is what God has called that person to be and to do. Here the biblical teaching about divine providence is presented in a particular and personal way. As far as Paul is concerned, divine providence is not something merely abstract and general, to be found only in a text-book of systematic theology, or to be discussed only in the classroom. What does God's providence mean? It means that it was no accident that Lydia was a seller of purple cloth, or that Aquila and Priscilla were tentmakers, or that Paul himself was a learned Pharisee.

It is tempting to regard such facts about people as trivial or inconsequential or 'unspiritual'. But for Paul they made up part of God's calling. Their particular gifts and aptitudes, their history, skills, friends and acquaintances, their contractual ties with others – all these factors, and many others, constituted that array of circumstances in which the Christian life was to be lived. Because these circumstances constituted God's calling it was their responsibility, upon becoming Christians, to be Christians *where they were*.

It was noted in chapter two that groups have arisen from time to time in the Christian church who wished to gain a deeper spirituality, or to express their discipleship to Christ more faithfully, by attempting to turn their backs on the everyday world. The monastic movement in the Middle Ages, religious ascetics and hermits, as well as some of the Anabaptist movements during the Reformation period, saw themselves as escaping from worldly entanglements to follow Christ more devoutly. It is necessary to emphasise not that such attempts failed but that they ought never to have been made in the first place. Such people saw spirituality in terms of place or community, not in terms of service and consecration.

As we saw Paul anticipated the mistakenness of such ideas in his teaching earlier on in 1 Corinthians. He told the church that he had written to them not to have anything to do with fornicators. But he had been misunderstood. What he had said was that the church was not to have anything to do with a *professed Christian* who is a *fornicator*. No one was even to eat with such a person (*1 Cor. 5:11*). But, Paul went on to say, he could not have meant that the Christians ought not to have anything whatsoever to do with any fornicator, or extortioner, or drunkard. He could not possibly have meant that, because in order to avoid contact with any such people it would be necessary to leave the world. Paul regards such an idea as both impossible and unnecessary. The Christian is in the world, but he is not of the world. To be in the world is part of his calling.

Paul's teaching finds support in Peter's first letter. We have already seen that in 1 Peter 2 Peter teaches that the Christian slave is to be different from the non-Christian in that when he is blamed because he is a Christian he is to take it not in a spirit of wounded pride, or by developing a martyr-complex, or by allowing resentment to fester, but 'patiently'. And, Peter adds, this is what he is *called* to (*v. 21*). A Christian's calling covers not only his job and the varied circumstances of his life, but also the need to suffer patiently as a Christian when it is necessary to do so. A person in such a situation is 'called' to follow in Christ's footsteps.

Paul and Peter are both teaching, in their doctrine of 'calling', that provided a person's manner of life is lawful, provided that he is not being forced to sin, the effectual call of God which makes a person a Christian should make no difference at all to the job he does. Christianity is not only compatible with a wide variety of circumstances but by God's grace and help, it is also able to flourish in them. A Christian's call by grace dignifies daily life, for such life is, or may become, a vocation. This idea of 'calling' holds the key, or at least one key, to a range of difficult and vexing problems, the problems of the relationship between a Christian's daily life in this 'present evil world' and his life before God.

THE DAILY LIFE AND THE SPIRITUAL LIFE

Part of the difficulty encountered in considering the relation between the daily life and the spiritual life lies in the fact that having once distinguished between the two, as many Christians are accustomed to do, it is very difficult to bring them together again. And so Christians frequently ask such questions as the following: Are these two 'lives' related simply by the different stretches of time devoted to each? One day in seven and parts of each other day for 'spiritual life', the remainder for 'daily life'? Does the spiritual life have to do with what is 'inner', with desires, motives, perhaps even dreams and visions, while the daily life is the life of education, natural skills, committees and things that we can handle and manipulate? Or is the spiritual life to be defined in terms of the lives of certain kinds of people – pastors or monks or missionaries? Theirs, it might be thought, is the ideal, the full Christian life. Theirs is the life, and the life-style, for Christians to copy! Other sorts of lives, the life of a civil servant or a decorator, say, are second best. They are ancillary workers. By asking the wrong questions the unity of the Christian life has been split apart. How can we put Humpty Dumpty together again?

The *beginning* of an answer to these questions surely lies in not setting up the problem in this way in the first place. For none of us lives two (or more) lives, but one life. When Paul wrote to the slaves and married couples of Corinth there is no suggestion that their problems were due to the fact that they were dividing up their lives disproportionately, that the daily life timetable was swamping the spiritual life timetable, or *vice versa*. Nor did Paul complain that they were failing to model their style of life on that of himself or the other apostles. Far from it. In fact, if anything the reverse is true (*I Cor. 9*). Rather, the problem lay in the *direction* of their lives. Their living was marked by an 'itch' for change that was driven on by a false view of spirituality and by what they had (mistakenly) come to regard as being God's will for them.

Since each of us lives only one life, our spiritual renovation must take place in the course of that life. It is not as if a person's spiritual life is encased in the daily life; rather, as each person lives his one life, his renovation, being remade in the image of God, takes place in that life. In this life there will be times which are more overtly 'religious', periods of worship, of Bible study, the enjoying of Christian fellowship, reflection and meditation. But these times are not to be sustained *at the expense of* the rest of our life, as if it were that only in these 'religious' situations is a person really living, while in the rest of his life he is simply ticking over. Working hard and creatively, or looking after one's aged relative, are activities which are equally Christian, which a Christian ought to want to do to the best of his ability. *Whatever* lawful thing the Christian does he must do to the glory of God (*1 Cor. 10:31*).

The question is sometimes raised as to whether a Christian who is a church member should be prepared to leave the church to work elsewhere to gain promotion. Some say he should not, on the grounds that his church membership comes first, while others say that he may, because the disruptive effects of such moves on the local church can be exaggerated. But the New Testament's teaching on 'calling' brings another perspective to the question. It is not simply a question to be decided by balancing effects or possible effects on the local church. What about the *job itself*, and a person's calling in it? Can it always be assumed that 'church comes first' and that daily work merely exists to provide a Christian with his living expenses?

[52]

But are not times of religious instruction and devotion to God in acts of worship 'better'? And if so, ought not a person to try to put as much time and effort into them as he possibly can, even if other matters are neglected? What about Mary and Martha? Did not Christ rebuke Martha for her busyness in housekeeping and say that Mary, who sat at His feet receiving instruction, had chosen the 'good part'? (*Luke 10:42*). He did, but it would be unwise to conclude from this single incident that Bible-study must always take precedence over housekeeping, and that dishes should be left unwashed and meals uncooked in order to spend more time at church or on one's knees. It is clear that the incident of Mary and Martha was unique, and that Christ's answer to Martha was provoked by her complaint, a complaint that was evidence of the fact that she was excessively busy and knew it. There is no suggestion in the text that Christ would have rebuked Martha had she not complained. And Christ did not rebuke Martha for being busy but for the complaint that Mary was not busy as well. What He said was not that such busyness was wrong, only that it was out of keeping, that Mary was making the most of present opportunities, and that Christ is best served not by feeding Him but by being fed by Him.

To see one's whole life as a divine 'calling' is both the key to Christian sanctification and the cement which holds together the various aspects of our lives, preventing them from splitting up into different, and disjointed, sealed compartments.

HUMAN LIFE AS A CALLING

According to 1 Corinthians 7 and 1 Peter 2 the idea of the Christian's 'calling' is a wide, an all-embracing one. It covers not only daily work, what one does in order to earn a living (Paul gives slavery as an example) but also family relations and friendships (Paul's example is marriage) and also what happened *before* one became an adult (Paul's example is circumcision). Each person, on being converted, is to remain in that 'calling'. Being converted, while revolutionary, is not itself a reason for breaking the web of relationships which exists at conversion. This web is a divinely-ordained field in which Christian renovation is to flourish, providing opportunities as it does for developing and learning the mind of Christ.

Paul also emphasises something else. The calling of God, the wider scene in which a person's effective call by grace is set, is also a 'distribution' made by the Lord in his sovereign wisdom. Not everyone receives the same distribution, but the Lord distributes differently to his people, as he sees fit (*1 Cor. 7:17*). This connects with Christ's teaching in the Gospels about stewardship (*Matt. 25:14–30*).

The thought of life as a divine calling, with the associated thought of stewardship, are biblical teachings which are largely absent from the Christian consciousness at present. It is not simply that the *word* has dropped out of use – though that fact is significant – but that a whole framework of thinking which the Bible invites Christians to use about themselves has vanished.

According to Scripture the whole of a person's life is fundamentally *serious*, something for which he is responsible before God, and for which he will have to give an account (*Rom. 14:12*). It is easy, in the modern world, to caricature such a view, to suggest that it means that Christians are to be long-faced and should emphasise individual responsibility before God to the point of neurosis. But to say that the Christian life is fundamentally serious does not mean that it is gloomy or morose. The Christian ought to be aware that he lives his life, the whole of it, before God and that he is individually responsible to God for what he 'makes' of it. Attempts are made to evade personal responsibility by blaming society or the media or advertisements or parents, but the Christian is to reject such explanations. And while he knows that factors such as sickness, weakness, ignorance and coercion of various kinds can lessen responsibility, and that responsibility can be shared, at work, in the family, among friends, and in the church, yet none of this can eliminate for him the conviction of his *individual* responsibility. It is basic for understanding life as lived before God. The life which I live before God is my life and I must give account for it. Basic to the Christian life, therefore, is a sense of individual responsibility before God from which all other responsibilities, duties and delights, are derivative.

The whole of life, with all its potentialities, is a gift from God. The contemporary emphasis is upon human rights and on the need to assert and to claim them. The Christian is not blind to his rights, particularly those that are enshrined in the law of the state insofar as those laws are in accordance with the law of God. Paul claimed such a right on a notable occasion (*Acts 25:11*), and one result of this was that he went to Rome as a Christian apostle (*Acts 28:30,31*). Yet the emphasis of the Christian life does not fall upon rights and their assertion but upon obligations and opportunities.

Life when understood as a calling from God also contains within it the conviction that lives are a divine trust from which we are not to attempt to escape. There is a widespread tendency to attempt to escape from bare reality through soporific entertainment, or through the attempt to get back to nature, or through various kinds of drugs and palliatives. But the life I live, with its various difficulties, unpleasantnesses, and its awkward facts, is nevertheless the life that I have been called upon by God to live. Its difficulties cannot be escaped, and it is part of the Christian's calling to attempt to handle them and to respond creatively to them. The emphasis of the New Testament is on the Christian's need to be sober (*1 Thess. 5:6*), to be wide awake (*Rom. 13:11*), and to be careful and watchful. These are not narrowly 'spiritual' characteristics, which apply to the prayer-meeting but not to the workplace, but they are to stamp the whole of a Christian's life.

It is a truism that each person is an individual, but it is often denied by an attempt to handle people in the abstract, as numbers, or 'souls', or a 'workforce' or by attempts to make all people conform to one particular psychological or social pattern. Christians ought to resist such pressures. The Bible's teaching about differences between people in the context of the affairs of the local church is quite clear. The local church is a body of which Christ is the head (*Col. 1:18*) and between the various limbs there are differences (*1 Cor. 12:14*) as well as interdependence, each limb contributing to the well-being of the whole.

But such differentiation goes beyond the life of the local church, according to Paul, and covers wider social and personal differences. The distribution of which Paul writes in 1 Corinthians 7 is not the distribution of gifts across the membership of the local Corinthian church (he touches on this, in the case of Corinth, in chapter 12), but the distribution of differences in life. So the Christian will resist pressures, either from within the Christian church or from outside it, to make people conform to a stereotype. A person to whom the Lord has not given the intellect of Einstein, or the torso of Hercules is not responsible for what he lacks, and he ought not to be consumed with anxiety or envy on that score. On the other hand he has been given certain gifts. God has called him to one kind of life, and it is for him to assess what that life is, and to live it responsibly before God.

THE REFORMATION AND THE IDEA OF CALLING

As noted earlier the idea of the Christian's life as a divine calling has all but vanished at present. Where the word 'vocation' is used it has a highly selective application, to nurses and doctors, and teachers perhaps, but certainly not to salesmen or housewives. But the idea of calling was very prominent at the time of the Reformation and immediately afterwards. It was one strand in the Reformers' attempt to show from Scripture that monasticism and the Roman Catholic belief that a priest was of a different order from other people was seriously mistaken and immensely harmful. Two extracts, one from Martin Luther and the other from John Calvin, will make this clear.

In 1520 Luther wrote *An Open Letter to the Christian Nobility of the German Nation concerning the Reform of the Christian Estate*. In this letter he developed an attack upon the teaching that the Roman Catholic clergy constitute a special class, the 'spiritual estate' while all other people – 'princes, lords, artisans and farmers' – form the 'temporal estate'. No, Luther in effect says, all Christians share the same faith, they are all baptised with the same baptism.

> Therefore, just as those who are now called 'spiritual' – priest, bishops or popes – are neither different from other Christians nor superior to them, except that they are charged with the administration of the Word of God and the sacraments, which is their work and office, so it is with the temporal authorities. They bear sword and rod with which to punish the evil and to protect the good. A cobbler, a smith, a farmer, each has the work and office of his trade, and yet they are all alike consecrated priests and bishops, and everyone by

[57]

means by his own work and office must benefit and
serve every other, that in this way many kinds of work
may be done for the bodily and spiritual welfare of the
community, even as all the members of the body serve
one another.

Luther was writing while accepting the mediaeval
assumption that the church and the state are co-extensive.
And yet his words also represent a profound break with
mediaevalism, a break which had enormous implications.
For Luther claimed that the distinction between the
clergy and the laity is not the distinction between the
spiritual and the temporal, but that the distinction is
simply a functional one. 'Everyone' – priest or cobbler –
'by means of his own work or office must benefit and serve
every other'. So a minister is not closer to God, he is not a
better or more worthwhile or more spiritual person, than a
cobbler or a smith. The difference between minister and
cobbler is functional: both are equal as believers before
God, both have worthwhile work, but that work is
different merely because each has a different gift and
opportunity. But each is called (Luther's word is not
'calling' but 'office') to serve God and one another in
society.

John Calvin, writing in a slightly later phase of the
Reformation, explicitly employs the idea of calling. In the
Institutes he wrote

For He (the Lord) knows with what great restlessness
human nature flames, with what fickleness it is borne
hither and thither, how its ambition longs to embrace
various things at once. Therefore, lest through our
stupidity and rashness everything be turned topsy-
turvy, He has appointed duties for every man in his
particular way of life. And that no one may thought-
lessly transgress his limits, He has named these various
kinds of living 'callings'. Therefore each individual has

his own kind of living assigned to him by the Lord as a sort of sentry post so that he may not heedlessly wander about throughout life . . . Accordingly, your life will then be best ordered when it is directed to this goal. For no one, impelled by his own rashness, will attempt more than his calling will permit, because he will know that it is not lawful to exceed its bounds. A man of obscure station will lead a private life ungrudgingly so as not to leave the rank in which he has been placed by God. Again, it will be no slight relief from cares, labours, troubles and other burdens for a man to know that God is his guide in all these things. The magistrate will discharge his functions more willingly; the head of the household will confine himself to his duty; each man will bear and swallow the discomforts, vexations, weariness and anxieties in his way of life, when he has been persuaded that the burden was laid upon him by God. From this will arise also a singular consolation; that no task will be so sordid and base, provided you obey your calling in it, that it will not shine and be reckoned very precious in God's sight.

As with Luther, there is more than a suggestion of mediaevalism here, the idea of a static society in which each person has a permanent place. No doubt also Calvin had in mind the social upheavals brought about by various Anabaptist groups and wished to distance himself from these. Nevertheless Calvin gives great prominence to the idea that each person's life is an 'assignment' from God, worthwhile in itself however modest, because it is received from God and is to be lived for God. And this fact, Calvin adds, is to act as a 'boundary', preventing over-much anxiety and care.

Extracts such as these from the seminal writings of the Reformation portray it as a kind of liberation movement, though one of a very different kind from the currently-fashionable 'liberation theology'. As Luther emphasises, the difference 'in kind' between clergy and laity, the clergy being 'spiritual' and the laity 'temporal', is completely without biblical foundation. There are not different kinds or orders of people, and certainly not different kinds or orders of Christians. All Christians are saved by the same Saviour, they are all equal before God, and they are all assigned various callings by Him, each (as Calvin pleads) equally legitimate and worthwhile.

Nor was the teaching that a person's everyday life is a divine calling a product of the Reformation that was quickly forgotten. An early and influential Puritan, William Perkins (1558–1602) wrote *A Treatise of the Vocations or Callings of Men* (published in 1603) in which the characteristic biblical and Reformed emphasis was upheld and developed.

> The action of a shepherd in keeping sheep, performed as I have said in his kind, is as good a work before God as is the action of a judge in giving sentence, or of a magistrate in ruling, or a minister in preaching. Thus then we see there is good reason why we would search how every man is rightly to use his particular calling.

Through the influence of Perkins and others the idea that a person's everyday life is a divine calling took root and became one of the characteristic marks of Protestant and more particularly of Puritan piety. Richard Baxter (1615–1691) devoted meticulous attention to it in his *Christian Directory* (1673). Another Puritan, George Swinnock, in his *Christian Man's Calling* (1661–5) provides characteristically systematic and thorough treatment of the theme, dealing with a person's calling in the family and in the home, at work, during times of adversity and prosperity, and so on. And in the final phase of Puritanism as a distinct movement, Richard Steele (1629–1692), another of the ministers who were ejected from their livings in 1662, wrote *The Tradesman's Calling* (1684).

Present-day circumstances are very different from those of the Reformers of four hundred years ago. And yet the temptations against which they warn are still with us. Sometimes such popular prestige is attached to work of a certain kind that nothing else seems worthwhile. Sometimes the work of the pastor is held up as a model, as the only worthwhile life-work for a Christian. But is this not precisely the clericalism against which the Reformers were warning? Sometimes there is snobbishness in society, even in the church. People are consumed with the need to make money and the thought of work as being intrinsically worth-while vanishes. Some take on too much responsibility. Of course there are problems. For example, how does the biblical (and Reformation) idea of life as a calling apply to those who are out of work?

Later an attempt will be made to look at some of these issues in more detail. But the basic thrust of the New Testament ought by now to be clear. The biblical teaching about calling cuts through all such attitudes. All lawful callings are equally valid and worthwhile, because each has God as its source and the service of God as its object.

CALLING AND SECULARITY

Much was heard some years ago about 'secular Christianity' and even 'religionless Christianity', based on the belief that it was an essential part of the Christian message that mankind had 'come of age' and no longer needed religion as a crutch. Such claims seem to have been largely forgotten.

While so-called 'secular Christianity' understood in these terms is largely a contradiction in terms, there is nevertheless, according to Scripture, a positive relationship between the Christian faith and 'the secular'. What matters, in deciding whether a particular calling is worthwhile, is not primarily what *kind* of work it involves, but the answers that it is possible to give to the following questions. Is the work lawful? Does it involve a person in sin? If not, then in what spirit is the work being done? Is it merely for personal ambition, or for the glory of God and the good of others, in response to God's love and mercy in Christ? If so, then, in the given set of circumstances in which a person is placed, is he making the best use of his talents, working efficiently, cooperatively, using his skills, making good use of time, and so on? These three conditions *define* the worthwhileness of work for the Christian.

This emphasis upon the worthwhileness of work of all types, the lawfulness of many different callings, has an important consequence. It prevents people identifying *one* particular job or profession or task with God's will – a kind of idolatry – since all lawful human interests are in accordance with God's will.

So the biblical analysis of work and daily calling is not based upon a dualism between the body and the soul, nor on one between the sacred and the secular, but between an inordinate love of self (a love that is opposed to love for God) and a love of God which is also a love of one's neighbour and one's self.

The 'two cities' (to use Augustine's phrase), the city of God and the city of this world, are invariably commingled in this life. Membership of the city of God does not mean that the Christian has no commitment to any earthly city. Nor is there an artificial separation, as in later Lutheranism, between membership of the kingdom of Christ, and the kingdom of men, as if the two never overlap or intersect. Rather the Christian ought to accept ordinary responsibilities and to carry them out for an ultimate end, the glory of God.

CALLING AND BIBLICAL WISDOM

The thought that the whole of one's life is a calling from God is not one which is peculiar to the Apostle Paul and to the Protestant Reformation. It is also characteristic of what is sometimes called the Wisdom literature of Scripture, and is particularly prominent in *Ecclesiastes*.

The biblical teaching that the fear of God is the beginning of wisdom is a puzzling and unattractive one to many because it is misunderstood. The fear of God is not the cringing, craven fear which a bully delights to create in others, but a respect and reverence for God on account of who He is, the matchless Creator, Lord and Judge of all. *Ecclesiastes* emphasises this theme. It is because God is the creator and the God of providence, the one from whom the whole of our lives derives, that men should – naturally – fear Him (*Ecc. 3:16,17. 8:6*). Human life is a serious matter, for it is life that is lived in the presence of God (*11:9*), with the gifts which He has provided (*2:24*), and in the light of the judgment to come when accounts must be rendered (*12:14*).

Not only can the fear of God be misunderstood, but what the Bible means by wisdom can also be misunderstood. According to Scripture the wise man is not someone who has superior knowledge or know-how or insight. It is not cleverness, or even experience, or the knowledge of secrets or mysteries, that makes a man a wise man. Nor is it organising ability and 'man-management'. Rather it is a person's recognition of his place before God, of his position as a creature, of his dependence upon God and his responsibility to God. The recognition of these basic facts, and the willingness to live in the light of them, is what constitutes biblical wisdom.

But even this, unfortunately, is liable to misunderstanding, for the idea of a person 'knowing his place' suggests a mediaeval society based upon the manor house, or the life of a Victorian English village. It was customary then for everyone to 'know his place' and common for the society to be frozen into immobility due to the distribution of wealth and poverty, to snobbishness and class-prejudice, and to the fear of change. But this (need it be said?) is not the biblical picture.

Scripture makes it clear that the fear of God, paradoxically perhaps, is not meant to freeze but to mobilise and liberate. The foolish man (in the biblical sense) is the person who thinks that he is himself the centre of the universe and that the whole of life revolves around him. He does not recognise his own limitations, and the way in which much of his life is taken out of his hands (2: 18–21). As a consequence the seemingly random and unjust occurrences of life frustrate him. He does not see his life as a divine calling, and he looks to its uncertain objects and events as the source of his happiness and blessing rather than to God the giver of them. As a consequence he is for ever being thwarted and is unhappy.

In contrast to this, the wise man lives in the present, using and enjoying what he has received as a gift from God. When *Ecclesiastes* says that there is nothing better for a man than that he should eat and drink and that he should make his soul enjoy good in his labour (2:24), this is not to be understood either as advice to 'eat, drink and be merry, for tomorrow we die', nor to live a life of fatalism, without energy and initiative. On the contrary, the advice is positive. It is contrasted on the one hand with the case of the man who has gained everything that his heart could desire but who lives without God (2:1–11), and on the other hand with the case of men who are continually frustrated by the failure of their plans, by the seemingly random happenings of life, and who are obsessed with the thought that anything they might achieve will not last. For who knows but what their achievements might not be squandered by a fool who shall follow them? (*2:18,19*).

Faced with such contrasting attitudes, what is to be the attitude of the God-fearer? The answer of *Ecclesiastes* is: there is nothing better than that a man should rejoice in his own works. Not for a moment is the Preacher suggesting an attitude of self-satisfaction, as though a person ought to attempt to boast before God about what he has attained. But in advising that a person should rejoice in his own works the Preacher is recommending the God-fearer to live in the present ('for who shall bring him to see what shall be after him?' *3.22*) and to find present delight and satisfaction in the full array of abilities, gifts and relationships which God the Giver has granted to him. This is 'his portion'. To attempt to thwart this, by trying to amass riches and to gain some kind of permanency and independence, or to imagine that any riches can be taken beyond the grave (*5:10–12, 5:15*), are not expressions of 'good sense' but of folly.

When the outlook changes and when the future cannot be guaranteed, what is a person to do? 'It is good and comely for one to eat and to drink, and to enjoy the good of all his labour that he taketh under the sun all the days of his life, which God giveth him; for it is his portion' (*5:18*). Earlier it was shown that, for Paul, a person's 'calling' was the whole network of relationships and opportunities and duties which formed his life. Now, in a very different setting, in the Old Testament, the same two themes are brought together. The wise man recognises all that he has and enjoys, his 'portion', as being that which God has given him, and he is to enjoy and use it to the full. He is to resist the pull of the past (*7:10*) and of the future (*9:10*). Whatever his hand finds to do – whatever God in His providence gives him to do – he is to do with all his might, recognising his own opportunity and responsibility.

[65]

So there is a world of difference between the man who lives only for this life and the man who recognises that the life which he has been given is God's gift, and who uses and enjoys it in that spirit. Superficially the two people may seem to live very similar lives. Yet the one lives *for* the present, neither acknowledging God nor even paying lip-service to Him, while the other lives *in* the present as his calling before God. Such a person lives in the present, not because the present is all that there is, but because the present is what God has given him, and he recognises that he is in God's hands. Life is haphazard, events seem to occur without rhyme or reason (although in fact they are all decreed by God) and the idea that human beings can 'plan' their lives in such a way as to iron out the unexpected and the seemingly random is a Utopian illusion (*8:14*). What then, is a person to do? Put tritely, he is to do what he can, to fear God, to live patiently before Him and for Him, and to use the opportunities God in His providence gives him with enjoyment and thanksgiving, as God's steward.

THE CALL TO THE MINISTRY

It may seem that with the stress that has been laid in this chapter on Paul's teaching that a person ought to remain in the situation in which God has put him, no place has been allowed for God's direct call of a person to a new situation. In particular, it may seem that no place has been allowed for the call to the ministry of the Word of God. The theme of the call to the ministry is a large one, but something ought to be said about it here both in order to allay possible misunderstanding and also to show how the idea of such a call fits in with Paul's more general approach.

The call to the ministry is *extraordinary*, not in the sense that it is miraculous, or accompanied by voices and visions, but because by it a man is taken out of many of the routine commitments of daily life. In particular he ought to be freed from the need to earn his daily living in order to give himself exclusively to the Word of God (*1 Tim. 5:17*). And so to be a minister of the gospel is not to pursue a career, nor is it to carry on a family tradition. No one is naturally in the ministry, or fitted for it.

The call to the ministry is extraordinary also in the sense that it arises out of the ordinary. The biblical pattern is that generally a person will carry on a normal calling, continuing in the place that God in His providence has put him, and it is when he is inwardly constrained to preach the gospel, and his gifts – his ability to handle Scripture, to preach, to give leadership – are recognised by the church, that his inward call comes to be outwardly ratified. It is as these inward and outward circumstances combine that a man has a warrant for leaving his regular calling and attempting to obtain a position of pastoral oversight.

The idea that every Christian ought to be in 'full-time Christian service', though intended to exalt the office of the ministry by attempting to copy it, has a tendency to devalue it. For instead of the ministry of the Word of God being regarded as a distinctive, high office to which a person is called from his daily calling, the assumption is that any well-meaning Christian can and should 'minister'. But if the price of a commodity is lowered then the demand for it will increase, and if there is a general belief that everyone ought to be some kind of minister, and that most people can be, then the character and quality of the ministry of the gospel will invariably deteriorate, as it has done in the present century.

The call to the ministry is unusual or extraordinary in a further sense. The minister is the ancillary or servant of the church of God (*2 Cor. 4:5*). While he is to lead, he leads by serving. And the aim of the ministry is not to give the impression to other Christians that they also ought to be ministers, or even that they are pale, second-best ministers, but to serve the people of God with the Word of God in order that in the situations in which they live they may be better Christians. For the normal Christian life – both statistically and in terms of the New Testament teaching – is not the ministry but the life of the disciple as a teacher or lathe operator or hairdresser or social worker. And the Christian ministry exists precisely to foster and encourage such discipleship. Thus the ministry should not be characterised by efforts to get people to leave their work or to treat it as second best but by self-effacingly aiming at helping believers to be more consistently Christian where they are, with all its temptations and pressures. It ministers the Word of God to them and thereby – with God's help – encourages the formation of the image of Christ in them (*Gal. 4:19*).

SUMMARY

For the New Testament, and for Paul in particular (because it is Paul who discusses these matters most directly), God's effective call of a sinner by his grace takes place within a wider setting than that of the individual's own 'spiritual life'. It takes place within a network made up of the individual character of the person, his relationships and his opportunities, and indeed of the total situation which makes him to be the person he is. One result of being effectually called by God's grace, of becoming a Christian, is that the believer comes to recognise that the existence of this network is not a matter of 'chance' but of God's providence. In God's wisdom, it constitutes the believer's 'calling' in a wider sense. Even those events in the past which a person on becoming a Christian may profoundly regret, have had an influence upon him which can be put to good use. They have not occurred accidentally, nor are they outside the over-arching purpose and plan of God. And so Paul the Pharisee, the educated persecutor of the infant Christian church, was able to use his gifts in the fuller understanding and exposition of the gospel of grace.

God's effectual call by His grace changes the way in which a person now regards his whole life. He sees it as a calling to be fulfilled for the glory of God, a theatre in which he is to engage in Christian warfare and in which the renewal of God's image in him takes place. It is the place where particular skills and aptitudes will be developed and particular traits of character formed, skills and traits that would not have developed in other circumstances.

Yet while a person sees his whole life as a calling, God's effectual call by grace also sets boundaries to the worthwhileness of that calling. A person's earthly life, his calling, is of great significance, but its worth is bounded and kept in place by the knowledge of the saving grace of God in Christ. Although the present life is important, it is not all-important, and Scripture repeatedly warns its readers by highlighting the tragedy of those who look for, and who gain, their reward in this life (*Matt. 6:2*). A Christian's present earthly life is not a *substitute* for God's grace in Christ, as in some versions of 'secular' Christianity. Not that it is altogether *unrelated* to it, as in pietism, but the Christian's present life is *consecrated to God* by the knowledge of His divine grace through Christ.

So God's effectual call by grace ought, properly understood, to make the one who is called regard the whole of the rest of his life as a divine calling. This is what the present chapter has been about, in an endeavour to make that connection clearer.

4: Calling and Freedom

We have already seen that the New Testament does not restrict the idea of God's call to the effectual call by grace, the call which makes a person a Christian, important as that call is. It extends the 'calling' of a Christian to the whole of a believer's situation in life – to the sort of family arrangements he has, his job or lack of a job, his place in society, even the lingering influences of his life before he was a Christian. All this constitutes a person's calling in the wider sense.

But there are further aspects to the biblical idea of 'calling'. Paul on one occasion reminds his readers, the Christians of the churches of Galatia, that they were 'called unto liberty' (*Gal. 5:13*). And Peter, though he does not explicitly use the language of calling thinks about Christian freedom in a similar way. He speaks of it as a gift of God which a Christian is responsible to use properly (*1 Peter 2:16*). And behind the teaching of Paul and Peter about freedom lies that of Jesus Himself, who came to proclaim deliverance to the captives (*Luke 4:18*), and to make people free (*John 8:36*).

In chapter one it was made clear that the liberation Jesus brought is not a liberation from political or social oppression but liberty to those who are in bondage to sin. The liberty they enjoy, therefore, is liberty from personal enslavement. It is a liberty that brings conflict as the 'new man', the Christian's regenerate self, and the unrenewed nature, battle against each other. But such conflict is a sign of life, and it will continue until the time when the Christian enjoys the 'glorious liberty of the children of God' (*Rom. 8:21*). The conflict arises because the Christian's newly-granted freedom is a freedom structured by the law of God. We shall now explore these matters further.

PAUL'S TEACHING

While the Christian's call to freedom is an extension of the idea of effectual calling, it would be a mistake to think that it is a separate event, something that occurs some time after the effectual call by divine grace. Rather it denotes a further aspect of effectual calling, that aspect which is concerned not so much with the causal power and sureness of God's grace in conversion, as with its end and final goal. As the Christian is called effectually *by* God's grace so he is called *to* freedom.

Freedom rings bells in the modern consciousness. As everyone wants to be 'reasonable' and to live in a 'democratic' society, so everyone wishes to be free. To be free from control, like a hot-air balloon soaring over the hills and roads beneath, is a modern ideal. A life without ties, without restraint, is thought to be the 'good life'. In the politics of nations such an idea expresses itself as self-determination, as freedom from colonial rule. In economics 'freedom' is translated as 'laisser-faire', in morals as permissiveness and the pluralism which allows a person to choose his own 'life-style', not to be dictated to but to decide for himself. In the background of all these expressions of freedom there may be the fear of dictatorship and of Victorian primness. For some, freedom even extends to anarchy in society and to the idea that there is no such thing as objective truth, but that each person is free to decide for himself what is true and what is false.

Perhaps it is needless to say that most of such suggestions both distort and impoverish the biblical, and especially Pauline view of the freedom that a person has in Christ. To see this more clearly it is important to study the contexts in which Paul's teaching about the Christian's call to freedom occurs.

One of these contexts is Paul's letter to the Galatians. Paul's overriding concern in writing to the Galatian churches was to prevent them from falling away from their profession of the gospel of God's grace in Christ which he had preached to them and through which they had become Christians. They were being seduced into believing that their salvation depended not only on what Christ had done as their representative in dying for them and being raised from the dead (*Gal. 1:4*), but also upon maintaining the Old Testament Jewish practices, not simply as commands of God to be kept, but as ways of gaining the favour of God. So Paul has two tasks. The first is to show that the Old Testament ceremonial law belonged to the pre-Christian era, and the second is to show that any attempt to add to the sufficiency of Christ's work for salvation is a perversion of the gospel, and is in effect 'another gospel' (*Gal. 1:6, 3:1, 4:9, 5:4*).

So Paul teaches that believers who live since Christ has come are freed from the divine obligation to keep the ceremonial law of God which the Judaisers were perverting into a way of salvation by human efforts. The original purpose of this ceremonial law was to act as a schoolmaster to preserve the integrity of the Jewish nation until Christ should come (*3.24*). In the situation before Christ came, Paul says that believers were like servants or immature children (*4.1*), being kept under the control of tutors and governors until the appointed time of Christ's coming arrived (*4:2–4*). Christ's arrival made the ceremonial law unnecessary, for it was the fulfilment to which the ceremonies pointed. His coming, and the coming of His Spirit at Pentecost, brought in new privileges for believers. For they experience sonship to God (*2.5–7*) in a way that Old Testament believers never did.

The Old Testament situation was one of bondage (*4:3*), for the people of God were kept in check by the elaborate and physically-demanding ritual of the Old Testament. Hence the folly of those who, having experienced New Testament freedom in Christ, desired to return to observe and to be in bondage to the 'weak and beggarly elements', keeping special days and requiring circumcision.

In order to enforce the contrast between the bondage of the Old Testament and the freedom of the New, Paul develops the history of Abraham, Sarah and Hagar as an allegory. Abraham had two sons, one by his bond-maid, Hagar, and the other by the 'free woman', Sarah (*4.22*). The son who was born of the bond-maid came as a result of Abraham's unbelieving impatience over the fulfilment to him of God's promise that he would have a son. Only the son whom Sarah bore, Isaac, was the son who came according to the divine promise. Paul says that Hagar is Mount Sinai, corresponding to the Jerusalem of his day, which remains in bondage, whereas the new Jerusalem is free. And as Ishmael, the child of the bond-maid, persecuted Isaac, the child of the promise, so those who urged the return to Old Testament practices were harassing the New Testament believers. But as Abraham was commanded to cast out the bondwoman and her son from his household (*4:30*) so, Paul implies, the New Testament Christians are to separate themselves from the teaching of the Judaisers. For Christians are, in effect, the children of the promise (*4:30, 31*).

What, then, is the liberty with which Christ has made New Testament believers free, a liberty to which they are called (*5:13*) and in which they are to stand fast (*5:1*)?

It is sometimes said that the Christian is 'freed from the law'. But this is a misleading and inexact answer. One reason is that 'the law' can mean different things. From Paul's argument it is clearly vital for the Christian that he is freed from any obligation to keep the *ceremonial* law, or to maintain the Levitical priesthood and its God-ordained arrangements. The Christian is freed from this law both as a requirement of God under the Old Testament order and more particularly from observing it as required by the Judaising perverters of the right use of ceremonial law. The reason why Paul is so emphatic is that if believers are circumcised with the intention of gaining the favour of God, then Christ would profit them nothing (*5:2,3*).

The demand of the Judaisers was a perversion of the original arrangement. It was never the will of God, in ordaining the elaborate ceremonial of the Mosaic era, in which circumcision was an integral part, to set up new conditions of salvation which a person might keep to justify himself before God. There is one covenant of grace in both the Old and the New Testaments, and the Mosaic arrangements marked a particular phase of that one covenant, and nothing more.

That phase ended when Christ came. So even if one can imagine Paul confronting not a Judaiser but a pious Old Testament believer he would still say to that person that since Christ, the anti-type of the Old Testament types, has come, there is now no need for the pious observance of these laws. They are out-of-date.

So, whether they are considered in their original intention, or as perverted by the Judaisers, the Old Testament ceremonial laws are done away with by the coming of Christ. And it is in these quite specific senses that the Christian is 'free', free from the obligation to keep the ceremonial law and therefore free from any possibility of perverting such obedience in a Judaising direction, as an expression of works-righteousness.

Are Christians 'freed from the law', then? Not exactly. They are free from the obligations of the Old Testament ceremonial. But does that mean they are free from all law? To discover the answer to this question it is necessary to look again at what Paul says. It is important not to attempt to answer this question in terms of some abstract theory but in accordance with what the New Testament actually teaches.

It is often convenient to distinguish, as we have done, between the *ceremonial* and the *moral* law when discussing the Old Testament arrangements. But it is important to remember that these laws are not two totally independent sets of laws given by God. The so-called ceremonial law is in effect a branch of the moral law, a God-ordained extension of the moral law as it applied to the church of God under the Mosaic dispensation of the covenant of grace. For as the moral law of God lays down the obligation to worship God only, and not to engage in any form of idolatry, so the ceremonial law showed *how* God was to be worshipped in that era. When that era passed, as it did with the coming of Christ, so the ceremonial law passed. But the passing of the ceremonial law does not mean the passing of all law. The Lord still commands men to worship Him alone, and to keep from idolatry. But how they are to worship Him must now take a distinctively New Testament form, as befits the New Testament era. As an old Scottish writer, John Brown of Wamphray, put it, commenting on Romans 8:3,4:

> by the Law here be understood that universal rule of righteousness which God prescribed unto men, and that certainly is the Moral Law, whereof, as to the Jews the Ceremonial and the Judicial were a part, or were reduced unto: and particularly the Ceremonial Law,

being God's instituted worship, they were obliged to observe it by virtue of the Second command.

But what does Paul say about the moral law of God and its permanent relevance? To find an answer to that question it is necessary to look at Galatians 5. But even before we examine this passage one thing is sure, that whatever Paul may say there about the moral law of God it is inconceivable that he will defend it as a means of salvation. For the whole of his previous argument about the impossibility of salvation by works completely rules out such a defence.

It is in Galatians 5 that the exact character of the liberty to which New Testament believers are called by God becomes apparent. Paul says that the liberty to which the Galatians are called – freedom from the Mosaic ceremonies – is not to be made an excuse by them for sinful living, living 'after the flesh'. Rather the Christians are by love to serve one another. Abandonment of the ceremonial law does not imply abandonment of all law.

So the liberty to which Christians are called is not a do-it-yourself vacuum into which the believer is free to put his own rules, or lack of rules, as he sees fit. Instead, it is a structured liberty. What the Christian is freed from – the obligation to keep the Old Testament ceremonial law – is quite specific, and what the Christian is called to is equally specific.

What is that structure? Paul is perfectly clear and explicit in the answer that he gives. The structure of Christian freedom is 'all the law'. Paul says that 'all the law' is fulfilled in the command 'Thou shalt love thy neighbour as thyself'. For having argued at length that all who are 'of the works of the law are under the curse' (*Gal. 3:10*), and having shown that the obligation to keep the ceremonial law of Moses has passed away in Christ (*chapter 4*), Paul nevertheless insists that the Galatians are so to conduct themselves as to love their neighbours as themselves (*Gal. 5.14*).

There is only one law that is summarised in this fashion, and that is the Decalogue, or more exactly the 'second table' of the Decalogue, those duties which concern the behaviour of one person with another. And so to 'walk in the Spirit' is to adhere to these standards; not to be 'under the law' (*Gal. 5:18*) as a means of justification, but at the same time not to 'fulfil the lust of the flesh' (*v. 16*).

So the Christian's liberty is shaped by the standards of the moral law of God. Paul's teaching is an endorsement of Christ's own teaching, that the 'second great commandment' is that a person ought to love his neighbour as himself (*Matt. 22:39*). And while Paul's stress falls on the second table of the law when he later lists the 'works of the flesh' (*vv. 19–21*) he specifically mentions idolatry which is an offence against the first table. There is a permanence about the moral law given by the Lord to Moses, endorsed by Christ, and now further endorsed by Paul.

In endorsing the law in this way Paul is not teaching that the Galatians, in walking in the Spirit, were fulfilling 'the spirit' of the law but not its 'letter'. They are not called to observe the moral law of God in some vague way in which the details do not matter. If this had been Paul's attitude he would not have provided a long list of seventeen items of the 'works of the flesh'. And in Romans 13, which is in many respects a parallel passage, Paul lists most of the commands of the second table (*v.9*), going on to say that all these commands are 'briefly comprehended in this saying, namely, Thou shalt love thy neighbour as thyself'. So the spirit of the law 'comprehends' the letter.

What then does Paul mean when he says that if a person is led by the Spirit he is not under the law (*Gal. 5:18*)? At first sight he seems to be contradicting himself, on the one hand teaching that the Christian is to love in accordance with the law while on the other hand teaching that the spiritual man (the Spirit-filled Christian) is not under the law. What can he mean? This verse is sometimes appealed to in order to create an opposition between 'spirit' and 'law', to teach that the Christian, as a spiritual person, is free from any requirement to keep the law. But this cannot be Paul's teaching, given what he teaches elsewhere. What, then, is he saying?

The phrase 'under the law' refers to the disastrously mistaken view which Paul opposed, that it is possible to justify oneself by keeping the law. All who take this view are 'under the law', recognising the law's authority, and believing (mistakenly) in the necessity to keep it for justification, and experiencing times of powerlessness and frustration as they realise that they cannot keep it. They cannot keep it, and yet they must, or God will not receive them.

If, in contrast, a person is led by the Spirit, then even though the flesh and spirit, the old nature and the new, are in conflict, nevertheless attempts to keep the law do not end in complete futility and frustration. Such a person delights in the law of God and is given a measure of strength to keep it. Because he loves God for what God has done for him in Jesus, he endeavours to keep the commandments of God, and hence the law is not an impossible burden or an insupportable yoke. There could not be a greater contrast than an obedience which arises out of delight in God and from a sense of His pardoning love, and an obedience which is a striving, in one's own strength, to gain the favour of God.

Paul's reference to walking in the Spirit and being led by the Spirit opens up another aspect of the freedom that the Christian has. For Paul is not simply teaching that the New Testament believer is free from the need to keep the ceremonial law and free from the deadly misconception that it is by law-keeping that a person is justified. Only to say these things – important as they both are – and no more would be the same as saying that the New Testament believer was in precisely the same position as any believer who lived before Moses and before the provision of the Mosaic ceremonial laws; Abraham, say, or Noah. But Paul is not teaching that the position of the New Testament believer is like that of Noah. He is at pains to stress that the New Testament church has, by comparison with the church under and before Moses, certain unique privileges. These privileges derive from the fact that the New Testament church comes into being some time after the coming of Christ and more particularly after the coming of the Spirit of Christ at Pentecost.

Paul's argument in chapter four of Galatians is that in the fulness of time God sent forth His Son to redeem those who were under the law. As a result of what Christ's death procured the redeemed receive the privilege of sonship (*4:4,5*). They are adopted into God's family, and although Old Testament believers were every bit as much believers as those in the New Testament they nevertheless lacked this privilege. They were children under bondage (*4:3*), or servants (*4:1*), not fully-mature sons. Because New Testament believers have sonship God has sent forth the Spirit of His Son, elsewhere called 'the Spirit of adoption'(*Rom. 8:15*), to ensure that the sonship is not formal but that the believers experience it in its fulness.

Adoption relates to freedom in a further sense, freedom as the regaining of the ability to do God's will that is lost as a result of sin and which was only very imperfectly experienced by the church under Moses due to the oppressive character of the law. So Paul argues that such an ability is not simply the gift of regenerating grace – for all believers in every era have such grace – but rather that it is the gift of grace in its peculiarly New Testament phase and development. Since Christ has come, and Christ's Spirit has been sent, regeneration has taken on new depths. Believers are no longer 'steered' by the complex ceremonial legislation, kept in check by it. They have the inner strength of the Spirit to enable them to do the will of God in a hostile world.

It is this liberty which Christ proclaimed at the outset of His ministry (*Luke 4:18*) and which He came to give to men (*John 8:36*), just as He taught that the coming of His Spirit after his own death, resurrection and ascension, would usher in a new era for His people (*John 14:26, 15:26, 16:13*).

So liberty in this sense is more a freedom *to* than a freedom *from*. Having stressed that the Galatian Christians in common with all Christians are freed *from* the obligation to observe the ceremonial law, and most certainly cannot be justified by keeping it, Paul stresses that Christians, led by the Spirit, are free *to* serve God in a way in which no believer before Christ was capable. Being united to Christ and empowered by his Spirit, a New Testament believer is freed from the demands of the ceremonial law as he is freed from the enslaving power of sin. For in Christ he sees more clearly what sin means (for it took Christ to the cross), more clearly than could be seen in the Old Testament. And in Christ he is given Christ's Spirit in a fuller measure than was the saint under the Old Testament, a Spirit who continually reminds the believer of what Christ has done and who gives strength for that 'faith which worketh by love' (*Gal. 5:6*).

Thus when Paul indicates that the Galatian Christians were called to liberty he has at least two different aspects of liberty in mind. On the one hand they were free from the rigorous demands of the Old Testament ceremonial, for Christ has come and fulfilled it. They were no longer servants, but sons. And on the other hand they have been given the Spirit of adoption which frees them from the power of lust, so that they are able to serve God in accordance with His will. Such freedom is, of course, imperfect, as Paul stresses. The flesh lusts against the Spirit, and the Spirit against the flesh (*Gal. 5:17*). Even in freedom there is the experience of conflict. More than this, such conflict is a sign of freedom, real freedom, for the believer is led by the Spirit and walks in the Spirit (*Gal. 5:16,18*).

FREEDOM AND RESPONSIBILITY

There is, so it seems, a third aspect to the liberty to which, according to Paul, the believer is called. A New Testament believer is free in the sense that he takes responsibility for himself. The Old Testament believer's life was hedged about by innumerable do's and don't's which affected every aspect of his existence, not only the elaborate and specific ceremonies of worship, but land and property, diet and hygiene. His life was programmed in detail. The New Testament stresses how physically burdensome and demanding such arrangements were (*Heb. 9:10, 10:1–3*) and how they were a sign of immaturity. As small children have to be told to do everything and have to be continually watched, sheltered, cautioned and disciplined, so had the Old Testament church. But now in the New Testament this burden has been lifted and replaced, not by a set of new burdens, but by renewed prominence being given to the principles of the moral law. Christians are invited to think for themselves and, inspired by the example of Christ, and indwelt by His Spirit, to apply these principles for themselves in the different details of their lives.

It is noteworthy that the New Testament gives explicit guidance in many areas of human life, and leaves the reader in no doubt that Christian responsibility extends to all these areas. Yet this instruction is given in the form of principles, or through highlighting Christ's character, or through letting us watch over Paul's shoulder as he deals with particular situations, or through combinations of all these ways. There is an absence of detailed regulation. And so believers and churches are invited to decide for themselves, not, it must be stressed, in a moral vacuum, but in situations in which the application of the moral principles is left to the believers who are invited to think for themselves. 'Judge ye what I say' is an important New Testament invitation (*1 Cor. 10:15*). Those who judge for themselves take responsibility for themselves in much the same way in which an adult takes responsibility for himself by comparison with a child, an illustration which the New Testament itself uses more than once (*1 Cor. 14:20, Eph. 4:14*).

THE SCOPE OF CHRISTIAN OBEDIENCE

The liberty to which each Christian is called is a *structured* liberty. The Christian life is not to be anarchic, a life in which a person makes up his own rules, or has no rules at all, as he goes along. Christian freedom is not only freedom from the oppressive obedience of the Old Testament and from the all-enslaving power of sin, it is also freedom to serve God whose service is perfect freedom. Such service ought, in the Christian, to arise out of sincere thankfulness for what God has done for him in Christ, and a desire for God's glory through his disciplined obedience.

But what is the scope of such service? How extensive is the obedient discipleship to which the Lord calls His people? It has been shown that both Jesus and Paul summarise the law in a similar fashion. Each calls upon men and women to love their neighbours as themselves

(*Matt. 22:39, Rom. 13:9*) just as each emphasises the obligation to love and serve the living God wholeheartedly (*Matt. 22:37, 1 Cor. 10:14–22*). It would seem, from such teaching, that both held that Christian freedom is to be structured and directed by the whole law of God, the Decalogue.

Even those Christians who accept the full authority of the New Testament are sometimes at odds over the place and the scope of the law in the Christian life, and this difference shows itself most acutely over the question of whether there is still an obligation upon Christians to observe one day in seven as a day of rest. Some take the abolition of the ceremonial law, and the coming of Christ, as meaning that the observance of one day in seven as a day of rest is no longer required in the New Testament era. Others maintain the continuity of the one-day-in-seven principle.

There are many books on the Lord's Day and I have no wish to turn this book into another such treatise. Nevertheless it may be useful to glance at this matter briefly, not only for its own sake but as a way of showing the position of the New Testament more generally on the scope of the law. I shall argue that from what the New Testament teaches about the continuity of the moral law it is reasonable to suppose that the principle of one day of rest in seven still continues. Besides serving to highlight the scope of Christian obedience this discussion will serve another purpose as well. For in view of the stress that later discussion will place on the part that daily work plays in the Christian's calling it is important to uphold the position that the obligation to work, apart from work of necessity and mercy, is to be restricted to six days out of seven.

If a survey is taken of those occasions on which the New Testament endorses the various commandments of the Decalogue the following position emerges. Besides those general endorsements of the law as a whole already noticed the writers of the New Testament explicitly endorse many of the other commandments. The references given in the list below are not exhaustive but illustrative.

First Commandment (*Luke 4:8*)
Second Commandment (*1 Cor. 10:14*)
Third Commandment (*Col. 3:8*)
Fourth Commandment (*Mark 2:27,28*)
Fifth Commandment (*Eph. 6:1–3*)
Sixth Commandment (*Rom. 13:9*)
Seventh Commandment (*Rom. 13:9, Gal. 5:19*)
Eighth Commandment (*Rom. 13:9*)
Ninth Commandment (*Rom. 13:9*)
Tenth Commandment (*Rom. 13:9*)

What is notable by its absence is any direct command to change the day of rest and worship from the seventh day of the week to the first day. There are no instances where the New Testament directly endorses such a changed fourth commandment as it does the unchanged remaining nine commandments. But neither are there any places in the New Testament where the change to the first day is directly forbidden. (Such texts as Rom. 14:5,6 and Col. 2:16 are usually and convincingly explained, not as references to the Jewish Sabbath, but to other days which were specially observed in the Jewish Calendar and were also called 'Sabbaths').

What are we to make of this omission? Some are quick to say that the absence of such explicit endorsement of the first day is equivalent to the principle of one day of rest in seven being no longer obligatory. A Christian *may* keep a day of rest, but he need not, they say. So the Christian is free to work on any day, and the only reason for keeping one day as 'special' is the weight of tradition and of practical convenience.

But is such a conclusion warranted? If nine of the ten commandments are endorsed by the New Testament during the course of the incidental teaching of Christ and the apostles, is it not reasonable to conclude that the tenth is endorsed as well, particularly if we are not told that the tenth is rejected? And is it not reasonable, given the New Testament teaching that Christ is Lord of the Sabbath (*Mark 2:28*), to conclude that the Apostles and the early church show by their practice that they believed that the change of day had the Lord's sanction? Although such an argument is not a conclusive proof that the commandment to keep the first day of the week as a day of rest is endorsed by the New Testament, it makes it reasonable to conclude this and at the very least to place the onus of proof on the shoulders of those who wish to maintain the opposite. This argument from the general endorsement that the New Testament gives to the Decalogue may naturally be supported by other kinds of evidence from the New Testament, particularly references to 'the Lord's Day' (for example, *Rev. 1:10*), as well as the call to the Christian to fulfil 'the righteousness of the law' (*Rom. 8:4*).

Granted, individual and social circumstances will differ vastly throughout churches which are 'internationalised' and which are not an integral part of the nation-state as was the church under Moses. These different circumstances will call for different responses as Christians strive to keep this commandment in the local conditions. Here once again is a situation in which, in a way that is characteristic of the New Testament, Christians are thrown back upon their own initiative. They are no longer servants, but sons.

It is reasonable to conclude, therefore, that the Christian ought to see the liberty to which he is called as structured by the whole moral law of God. His liberty is expressed as he seeks to apply these principles in changing and differing circumstances.

THE LAW OF GOD AND OTHER PEOPLE

The liberty to which each Christian is called is a personal liberty, freedom from any personal obligation to keep the ceremonial law of the Mosaic era and, by God's help, free from the all-enslaving character of sin. But the Christian does not live in a world of his own, nor does he live merely with other Christians in a religious enclave. He lives 'in the world', mixing with others who do not share his outlook and standards and who in some cases are markedly hostile. His conduct will affect them as theirs affects him.

How is the Christian to proceed? In such circumstances it is important to bear in mind that the law of God which structures the Christian's liberty, and which provides the rule of his living, is not imposed arbitrarily. The law reflects the character of God ('be ye holy, for I am holy') and it is for the true good of His creatures, those made in His image ('that it might be well with thee'). Some theologians have so emphasised the divine sovereignty, including especially the sovereignty of the divine will, that they have made it appear that God could, simply by an act of the will, have commanded or forbidden anything. God could have commanded adultery, they say, and then adultery would have been good, and chastity evil. He could have permitted stealing, and then stealing would have been allowable.

But there is no biblical warrant for such speculations about the divine will, or for these conclusions. When the Bible proclaims God's goodness, His love and mercy, as well as His justice and His wisdom, these characteristics are inseparable from God Himself. It is impossible for Him to lack any of them and still be God. And when, for example, the Bible refers to the 'goodness' of God, what is meant by that term is related positively to what we mean when we talk of human goodness. To suppose that God might, by an arbitrary act, decree what is not in accordance with His supremely good moral nature, is unthinkable. And to suppose that the moral character of God bears no relation to what we regard as moral goodness, is also unthinkable. The Bible emphasises that the moral character of God is seen supremely in Christ. No doubt many of God's ways are mysterious to us because of human ignorance and wilful blindness, but they are not mysterious because what the Bible calls God's goodness is really wickedness, or because what the Bible calls God's mercy is really implacable hatred.

And yet there are times when the Bible functions as a *corrective* to the prevailing views of what is good and right. People are not to conclude, hastily, that what they normally or customarily think of as being instances of goodness or justice are what God also thinks of in this way. Human standards, which are liable to be warped by sinful prejudice, have to be corrected by biblical standards. And yet the biblical standards are not arbitrary but set forth standards which, if they are followed, benefit men and women.

These matters may seem abstruse to some, while being blindingly obvious to others. But it is necessary to stress them because of the widespread misconception that Christian standards, those standards which are expressed in the moral law, are only for Christians and that others who are not Christians cannot be expected to benefit from them. Such a misconception is sometimes fostered by Christians themselves, but more particularly by the widespread modern belief that moral standards are relative to a time and culture, and that there are no overriding and objective moral standards. But Scripture shows that moral standards are as objective as God Himself, and that though God might from time to time have required

[87]

particular observances, as in the case of the ceremonial law, yet the underlying moral law of God expresses abiding standards which are for the enduring benefit and blessing of mankind in general.

The Christian lives in a situation in which the 'common grace' of God restrains the sinful tendencies of men so that their actions are in accordance with at least some of the law of God some of the time. Even 'barbarous people' are able to show kindness (*Acts 28:2*); Paul is able to use his rights as a Roman citizen (*Acts 25:11*); people who have never heard of the law of God are nevertheless able to act in accordance with it (*Rom. 2:14*); and the state exists for the punishment of evil-doing and the reward of those who do well (*1 Pet. 2:13,14*). What these scattered pieces of evidence from the New Testament show is that human life continues in a bearable and worthwhile manner because God preserves in people a recognition, even a half-formed recognition, of His law and of the benefits of observing it.

This is the world in which the Christian lives. It is a world which is sometimes hostile to him and yet Scripture shows that his Christian conduct, his living in Christian freedom, is not something which is totally alien to this world. He will be able to benefit from society in general and in turn be able to benefit it.

Paul could well have had such matters in mind when in Galatians 5 he lists the 'fruit of the Spirit' – love, joy, peace, long-suffering, gentleness, goodness, faith, meekness, temperance – and adds, 'against such there is no law' (*v. 23*). Not only are Christians who manifest such fruit free from the power of the law to condemn, no longer living in fear of its judgment, but also there is no law which could fault conduct which is in accordance with such standards. No system of law could, practically speaking, outlaw the virtues which Paul lists here;

instead it requires them, or at least conduct which is in accordance with them, otherwise no society of people could exist.

And so the liberty of the Christian's calling is not a liberty which frees him from the world. On the contrary it takes him into the world, a world which is sometimes openly hostile to the claims of Christ, but which needs, paradoxically, the standards which the Spirit of Christ bears as fruit in the lives of Christians if it is to continue functioning as a society and not to collapse into utter lawlessness. The Christian may thus expect some beneficial consequences of his conduct to be recognised even by those who are not Christians. His conduct will be of use to them, even if the recognition they give to it is grudging and often accompanied by indifference or hostility to Christ Himself.

FREEDOM AND SUCCESS

Everyone wants to be free, and the promise of freedom has an enormous appeal. But 'freedom' is a many-sided word. Already we have noted two senses in which the Christian is free. He is free from the demands of the Old Testament ceremonial law, and he is free from the all-pervading enslavement of sin. But are there more freedoms that the New Testament promises and that a Christian may expect?

Here it is necessary to be careful, and to draw a distinction between what is *essential* and what is *desirable*. The two freedoms that we have been highlighting are essential. They are part of what it means to be a Christian. Anyone who is not benefiting from them has a reason to be seriously concerned about his position, just as Paul was concerned about the Galatian churches which had been bewitched by the Judaisers. But what about freedom of public worship, and freedom from health and from financial worries? Are these also to be expected? Are they essential?

Freedom to worship in public is desirable, but it is hardly essential. Such freedom is to be prayed for, and worked for. The church is commanded to pray God that He will so order political and social circumstances that Christian people will be able to lead quiet, peaceable, godly and honest lives (*1 Tim. 2:2*). To have such freedom is itself a great blessing, not only in the opportunities that it gives for unhindered worship and evangelism, but also for the other freedoms that it brings in its train, as the history of toleration in the British Isles and elsewhere shows. But although toleration is a blessing, it is not an inevitable blessing, as times of slackness and indifference and 'moderatism' in the life of churches also show. Nor is it essential. Churches have remained faithful and fruitful even when faced with hostility and persecution.

Do these remarks also apply to freedom from financial worries and from the blight of ill-health? Here it is necessary to be even more cautious and careful, particularly in the face of the claims that some religious leaders make that the Christian gospel is a 'gospel of success', that financial prosperity and bodily healing are part and parcel of the gospel which a Christian has a right to expect and to enjoy by faith in God. Is it true that if you pray to God He will make you rich? Need a Christian be sick?

It goes without saying that good health is an enormous blessing, and the Christian, along with everyone else, can be thankful for the availability of health care and for every new beneficial advance in medicine. The Christian will be keen to support research and other efforts in these areas, for such advances are part of the subduing of the creation to which mankind is called. It is no accident that many of the early pioneers in modern medicine were Christians.

The Christian will also acknowledge that God in His providence may work to cure a person's ill-health. But is good health essential to the gospel in the sense that someone who suffers sickness is for that reason shown not to be a Christian or not to be a faithful Christian? Is all sickness due to unbelief or to specific sin which if confessed will result in immediate healing?

It is clear from the New Testament that it is not. For there are occasions when the Lord in His wisdom brings sickness in order to teach that His grace is sufficient and that His strength is made perfect in bodily weakness (2 *Cor.* 12:9). So ill-health, which is generally a curse, may be a blessing. For this reason when a Christian prays for good health he cannot plead any divine promise which guarantees that his prayer will be answered. Instead he must pray 'if it be Thy will'.

Similarly with financial and business success. It is natural perhaps that matters which the surrounding popular culture values so highly should invade the church. But the idea that God will make a person rich if he has faith is as pernicious in its way as is 'liberation theology'. Perhaps it is true that as a Christian works hard and lives frugally he may expect to accumulate wealth. But the Bible warns emphatically against the dangers of riches, of the way in which wealth can take the heart from God. It warns of the uncertainty of earthly riches (*1 Tim.* 6:17). The prosperity of the wicked is held up as a warning (*Ps.* 73). The Christian is to learn to live a day at a time, to learn how to abound and how to be abased, to be a faithful Christian in times of adversity and in times of prosperity. With wealth comes, almost invariably, a love of luxury, and yesterday's extravagancies come to be expected as today's essentials. These words of R. L. Dabney are surely timely for any Christian who lives in the midst of twentieth-century affluence:

We profess a difference between ourselves and the unrenewed, as radical as that between light and darkness, almost as wide as that between heaven and hell. But in all visible and practical concerns which interest the unrenewed heart, we nearly resemble them. Our words say that we believe riches to be vanity and emptiness. Our acts seem to say that we love and seek them as intensely as those do who make them their all and their god. We say in words that 'we have here no continuing city', but in act are as eager to adorn our dwellings here as though they were our only home. We profess that we have richer and nobler enjoyments than the pomp of this life, and then swell and rustle with as much pomp as any other human insect of a day. What is the result? The world believes our conduct and not our words, like a shrewd world as it is.

So there are different kinds of freedom; some are intrinsic to the Christian's calling, some are desirable, and those that are generally desirable may also carry dangers with them. They may be denied to the Christian in accordance with the wisdom and goodness of God. And as we noted earlier, far from the Christian being invariably called to 'success', measured in terms of bodily health or financial wealth, he may be called to unspectacular but costly suffering for Christ's sake in a pattern of faithful endurance which shadows Christ's agony for sinners.

SUMMARY

When a person becomes a Christian he is effectively called by God's grace in a unique set of personal circumstances which constitute God's calling in a wider sense. God calls him through these circumstances to live one unified life to His glory. In the present chapter we have seen that the Christian's calling is a liberation, a structured liberation in which he is called to faithful discipleship. The New Testament believer is not a slave or an infant but he is called as a son of God indwelt by the Holy Spirit to apply the commands of his Father to the manifold, changing and often unpredictable circumstances of his life in the world. In these circumstances daily work takes an important place, as the next chapter will make clear.

5: Work and Calling

Within a Christian's wider 'calling' work plays an important part. The Bible teaches us that daily work is not the result of sin, but that it is part of the divine mandate for mankind (*Gen. 1:28*). Eden was not a pleasure park, but a garden to be maintained by human labour. Mankind is created to know and to serve God, and part of the way in which God is to be known and glorified is through daily work. He is honoured as the needs of men are met through the tapping of the resources of the creation. And so, while the difficulty of work, the laboriousness and the sense of futility which often accompanies it, is due to sin, work itself is good. As with all other aspects of the creation, however, work is under the curse. This does not make it a totally useless activity, for in the goodness of God much human work is purposeful and satisfying. But it does account for the frustration and social division that often accompanies the need to work.

For the Christian, called by grace, daily work is part of his over-all calling. For he is called to be re-creative, and it is as his character develops in work, and as the products of his labour, whether goods or services, are found to be useful to his fellows, that God is honoured. This chapter offers an understanding of work from this perspective, one which attempts to integrate work and Christian discipleship together.

The character of the good news of the gospel and the way in which that goodness is to be received by men has important implications for the way in which life is to be lived after a person's conversion. Suppose that the good news of the gospel could be 'administered' to a man by a drug or soporific which, in a dream-like way, detached him from the world. Suppose he could float off into a visionary world, a fantastic state of rest and peace and bliss. It might be expected that, under these circumstances, the 'ideal life' would be one of detachment from life and from everyday affairs. Many cultic religions which use drugs are of this form.

Or suppose again that the gospel taught that what matters supremely is the human spirit or soul and that the body and all that involves the body – food, rest, exercise, sex, clothing and shelter, pain and healing – are of no importance. Then it might be expected that commitment to the gospel would require detachment from the body and all its concerns and that the 'ideal life' for the Christian would be one of denial and asceticism, a life in which the body was neglected and subdued.

These thought-experiments may help us to understand the nature of the Christian gospel more clearly. For the gospel is not a drug which sends people to sleep, to enjoy a blissful dream-world. Rather, it is a presentation of God's truth which requires alertness of mind, a person's full attention. Conversion is not like falling asleep but being awakened from sleep (*Eph. 5:14*). God's calling is not a case of life running down; it is new life, a new birth, a new creation (*1 Pet. 1:3*). All the imagery that the Bible uses to convey to us what the divine calling by grace is like strongly suggests that a person is not put to sleep by the gospel, but brought to reality. It is not the Christian who lives in a dream world but the non-Christian. God's grace in Christ enables a person to see himself, and his relation to God, and to other people, as these things really are. The Christian comes to recognise this by having new life brought to him so that the blindness and the distorting effects of sin are substantially removed. Hence the call of God often has disturbing effects, for it requires a person to undergo a whole reorientation in life.

Again, as we saw in the last chapter, the call of God does not only awaken the mind. It is a serious mistake to suppose that the Christian gospel requires a person to neglect his body. Rather it stresses that the body is a divine creation as much as the soul, that in order to redeem mankind the eternal Son of God took human nature, becoming embodied, that He is for ever united to human nature in glory, and that at the last there is to be a resurrection of the body without which Christ's redeeming work would be incomplete (*1 Cor. 15*). The idea that the Christian gospel has nothing to do with man's body, and that this is what makes it 'spiritual', is a complete misunderstanding.

The nature of the gospel is such that there is nothing about it, either in its content or in the way in which it is presented, to suggest that working and living a life in the world is unworthy of the gospel or that it is second-rate and unspiritual. In fact, the reverse is true. The believer, effectually called by grace, is made an embodied soul, a unity, in God's image. He is in God's world, growing up in a family, with work and other commitments. He has a mandate from God to subdue the creation for God's glory. And the gospel clears his mind and strengthens his resolve to fulfil that mandate.

WORK AS PART OF THE CHRISTIAN'S CALLING

While the whole of a person's life constitutes his 'calling', work is an important part of that calling. In 1 Corinthians 7 Paul takes up the case of a slave who was so impressed by the fact that he was now a Christian, that he was tempted to think that this change over-rode all other commitments. For after all what are human obligations and relationships in comparison with the new relationship with Christ? The slave was owned by another man. Does not the gospel dissolve that relationship? Paul denies this. That relationship, and the work it involves, is part of that person's calling. There is nothing intrinsically unworthy about it and, provided that his master does not force him to sin, there is nothing about it which is inconsistent with the Christian gospel.

It is possible, without getting involved in the question of whether the Bible teaches the permissibility of slavery, to see a principle at work. If Paul directs a slave to stay where he is on becoming a Christian, *how much more* ought a person who is employed under modern conditions of employment to stay where he is when he becomes a Christian.

The argument that Paul uses to support his direction to the slave is at first sight a surprising one. He says that the slave is Christ's freeman, just as a Christian who is not a slave must remember that nevertheless he is Christ's slave (*1 Cor. 7:22*). What does Paul mean? He is emphasising that even in a state of slavery the freedom to serve God remains, while in the case of a Christian who is not a slave he is not free merely to do as he likes, but he is Christ's servant.

Paradoxical though it may seem, Paul is using the fact that the Christian is united to Christ – the most basic and precious relationship – as an argument *not* for the overthrowing or repudiating of all other relationships, but as an argument for maintaining them, or as many of them as are consistent with the moral and spiritual demands of the gospel. It is the very fact that Christian freedom and service is more basic than all other freedom and service which gives new perspective to these other sorts of service, other aspects of the calling, and requires the Christian to retain them.

So if being a slave could be part of a person's *calling* as a Christian, how much more (a twentieth-century Christian may tell himself) is the job that I presently occupy as a Christian. It is the gift of God's providence. It is what He has in His sovereign wisdom 'distributed' to me. So work is part of a Christian's calling.

It is not the only part, of course. The Christian is not called to be a workaholic, someone for whom *only* his work matters. What makes for difficulty for the Christian is that there is not one supreme duty which he has to fulfil but there are numerous competing duties and interwoven relationships each of which claims time, energy and commitment. But one relationship may help another, offering support and strength, as marriage may support work, and work marriage. On the other hand they may compete with each other, and a Christian will have to think seriously about which obligations, in a certain set of circumstances, come first. Ought he to work overtime, or to be at home with his wife and family?

Work is part of a Christian's calling, part of his 'vocation'. As we saw earlier this biblical idea has had a profound influence in Europe and North America since the Reformation but has largely been forgotten, due to the eclipse of the influence of the Christian gospel from national life, or has been distorted through ridicule and caricature. But with such strong biblical backing Christians at least ought to resist the fashion and attempt to re-instate the idea of 'calling' in their own lives and those for which they have some responsibility.

Work considered as an important part of the Christian's overall 'calling' brings together a number of features. In the first place the Bible gives great prominence to the idea that human lives are lived in the sight of God, and this thought includes a Christian's daily work, as Paul explicitly notes when he reminds Christians that they have a Master in heaven (*Eph. 6:9*). It is not that the 'spiritual/religious' part of a man's life must be lived before God, those times when he is on his knees, or reading the Bible, and that the remainder of his life is his own affair. The basic motive for serving other men in work is that one is a servant of God.

A Christian's work is not therefore 'just a job', something burdensome which he attempts to make easier by being slipshod or second rate. It is part of his calling, his service to God. Yet this may at first seem rather ridiculous. How could a person whose job it is to serve dinners at school, or to make parts for sewing machines, or to manage people on a factory floor, be serving God? Is not such language merely religious rhetoric? Is it not pious talk which amounts to little? Such language *can* merely be pious talk but it need not and ought not to be. According to Scripture the plain truth of the matter is that work is an important part of the divine calling of each Christian. In serving others through his work the Christian is serving God, honouring Him by faithful stewardship. For through the work that God in His providence has assigned to him the Christian is attempting to glorify God. Such talk becomes merely pious when it is romanticised and separated from biblical convictions about divine providence, about life lived in the sight of God and about the judgment to come.

So work is not, for the Christian, simply a means of 'earning a living', 'keeping body and soul together' as it is sometimes put. It is that, of course, but it is more than that. The fact that there is work to do, and that people are able to earn enough to eat and to provide for themselves and their families, is itself a blessing from God. But the idea that work is an activity from which something else –

money – can be extracted, and that if the money was not needed there would be no obligation to work, is not a biblical idea, however current it may be in western society.

It is unbiblical because it detracts from the belief that a person who is working is serving God *in* the work that he is doing, and that there is something intrinsically correct and worthwhile in carrying out a piece of work for its own sake or for other reasons besides money. The assumption behind the attitude which sees work only in terms of earning money is that a person is only serving God truly in his leisure-time activities, or that he is only serving God in those activities which he has deliberately set himself to do, his 'discretionary time'. The thought that a person is serving God in situations which the providence of God *lays upon* him, which he has not explicitly chosen, but in which he finds himself living, is not a popular idea, but it is biblical.

The teaching that work is a divine vocation, and that satisfaction, the satisfaction of serving God is bound up in it, will meet with one obvious objection. What if the work is demeaning, or trivial or boringly repetitive, or if it is carried out in difficult or unwholesome conditions? Surely it is not reasonable that a person, even a Christian, who is trying to serve God in his calling, should think that God is served in a situation in which a person works under such conditions. Is it really being suggested that, in the name of fulfilling a divine calling, a Christian should put up with this?

GIFTS AND OPPORTUNITIES

Work is often repetitive and trivial, and much of it seems pointless. Best efforts often lead to frustration. How should a Christian respond to such facts?

In the first place it must be recognised that people differ from one another. One important aspect of Paul's reasoning about the divine calling is that of a divine 'distribution' that varies from person to person. This idea echoes the teaching of Christ in a number of the parables (e.g. *Matt. 25:14–30*). Such a distribution not only means that people have different situations in life, but also that they are differently equipped, by ability and temperament, to deal with those various situations. It is a trite point to say that people are different, and yet it is something that Scripture emphasises. So that what to one person is intolerably boring and repetitive may not be so to another, for he may be the sort of person who is happiest with a predictable routine. He may need to know exactly where he is and what is required of him. Similarly what is challenging to one person may put intolerable pressures on another person who is not used to making decisions, or to taking initiatives and accepting individual responsibility for his success or failure. For some such responsibilities are of the very essence of work, they are what make it worthwhile, while for others such tasks are simply 'beyond them'.

It is important to realise that such differences, of themselves, are of no spiritual or moral significance whatsoever. No guilt attaches to a person because he cannot take responsibility, just as no special merit accrues to one who is able to do so. Western society seems to put a special value upon individual personal success, where this is measured in terms of individual initiative, responsibility, drive and energy, with the 'consumerist' life-style that goes with it – clothes, cars, holidays and the like. Such ultra-competitiveness can be personally crushing to anyone who cannot succeed in these terms, and a person may feel guilty that he is not able to sustain this kind of life. But the biblical teaching is clear. There is no need to feel guilty. No law has been broken. The fact that a person cannot achieve such a life-style is not a sin, and such a way of life may itself be a snare (*1 Tim. 6:9*). 'Success' in God's sight must not be measured in terms of the worldly criteria of success. A Christian is called to do what he is best fitted to do in the total situation which is God's 'gift' to him. Hard as it may be to realise the fact, such biblical teaching ought to have a releasing and liberating influence upon anyone who is burdened by the pressure to conform to some 'type' which is derived not from Scriptural patterns of living but from the colour-supplement magazines.

Contentment with one's situation, and a determination to work faithfully and vigorously in it to the best of one's ability, is the basic biblical stance. To live like this is to fulfil one's calling. And yet the biblical teaching does not mean that a person may never change his work, or move house, or retire. One taunt of Karl Marx against religion in general and against Christianity in particular was that it is a 'halo of the vale of woe', a means of getting people to be reconciled to a situation in which they are being exploited. As Marx understood things, religion – and particularly the hope of heaven – compensates the exploited and oppressed with the thought of an eternal reward to counterbalance present inequities.

There are several errors in this analysis but the most important one is the assumption that the Christian ought never to seek change – either personal or social change – but passively to accept his 'lot' as something he is fated to endure. While the Christian ought never to lend support to any revolutionary activity which attempts to overthrow the established political order in which he lives – since the 'powers that be' are ordained by God (*Rom. 13:1*) – nevertheless the New Testament teaching about gifts and opportunities clearly implies that when an opening presents itself (i.e. when God in His providence presents it) in which a person judges that his gifts and talents will be better used, and the change does not involve him in the sin of neglecting some present duty, then he may seize the opportunity. This is Paul's explicit teaching in 1 Corinthians 7. Writing to the Christian slaves, he advises them to remain in their calling, adding that if they have the opportunity to obtain their freedom then they may (not 'must') take it (*1 Cor. 7:21*). And so the Christian is not deep-frozen into some caste from which he may never escape.

John Calvin, whose views on the idea of 'calling' quoted earlier may seem to be rather static, comments on Paul's teaching as follows

> It might seem as though the words conveyed this idea, that every one is bound to his *calling*, so that he must not abandon it. Now it were a very hard thing if a tailor were not at liberty to learn another trade, or if a merchant were not at liberty to betake himself to farming. I answer, that this is not what the Apostle intends, for he has it simply in view to correct that inconsiderate eagerness, which prompts some to change their condition without any proper reason, whether they do it from superstition, or for any other motive. Farther, he calls every one to this rule also – that they bear in mind what is suitable to their *calling*. He does not, therefore, impose upon any one the necessity of continuing in the kind of life which he has once taken up, but rather condemns that restlessness, which prevents an individual from remaining in his condition with a peaceable mind, and he exhorts, that everyone stick to his trade, as the old proverb goes.

Work, paid employment, is a central part of the Christian's calling and he must seek, under God, opportunities to utilise his talents. But the reason for this may still not be as clear as it ought to be. The reason is not simply that the Christian ought to be efficient and effective in his work, but that he ought to look for satisfaction *in* his work, and attempt, in the course of his employment, to discover and implement ways in which his work can be more rewarding, enjoyable and useful for himself and others. So strong is the current idea that work is a necessary evil, that it is opposed to leisure and to 'the week-end', or that it is opposed to the more 'spiritual' activities of prayer and praise, that it is extremely difficult to recognise that the Christian ought, as part of his calling, to find intrinsic satisfaction in what he is doing. This is not merely the satisfaction of knowing that in doing the work he is doing God's will, but satisfaction *in the work itself*, in using his talents, however modest, in developing the possibilities of his calling.

The Bible tells us that the Lord takes pleasure in His creation (*Gen. 1:31*) and in the redemption of the Church through Jesus Christ (*Eph. 1:5*). And the glorifying of God consists largely in the display of God's character in various different activities. As a Christian a person is called on to be re-creative, to become, as Adam was, God's steward; and one of the ways in which this creativity is exercised is in the use and development of those various powers and combinations of powers that God has given to him. The Christian honours God when, like God Himself, he takes pleasure in what he does.

DISCIPLINE AND DUTY

A further way in which the Christian's attitude to work and to his 'calling' may be approached is in terms of a person's obligation to God and to his neighbour, a way which does not contradict what we have already seen, but complements it.

There have been times in history when the idea of duty has become so dominant that it has swallowed up every other reason for acting, and has been taken to absurd and even to sinister lengths, for example, the Prussian idea of duty to the state and the way in which this became demonic and idolatrous in Hitler's National Socialism. But at present, perhaps as an understandable reaction against Nazi terrors, there is the opposite danger of dismissing the idea of duty as a reason for any action at all. Such an attitude has infected the Christian Church, as can easily be seen by the popularity of the idea that to have duties, and to do things out of a sense of duty is 'legalistic' and demands a spirit and an outlook on life which is entirely out of keeping with the basic thrust of God's saving grace in Christ. For did not Christ bring a message of love? How can such a message have anything in common with duty?

But such opposition between love and duty is ill-advised. It was shown in an earlier chapter that the Christian is called to freedom as a result of his effectual call by grace. He is no longer condemned by the law, he is freed from the myth and misconception that his justification before God depends upon actions that he can perform in his own strength to please God or to merit His favour. He is given new desires and motives to serve God from love and devotion for what He has done through Christ.

And yet, for all that, he is also *bound* to God, as Paul puts it (*1 Cor. 6:20*). Such a bond is of the very essence of *religion*. And so what a person may *want* to do, even what a Christian person sometimes may want to do, is not necessarily a true measure of what he *ought* to do. What God requires of Christians comes as a recognition of the obligation not to serve God in order to merit His favour, but to serve God out of gratitude. Yet the standards of service are God's, and the Christian must resist the temptation to substitute his own standards, or to assume that his own standards *are* God's standards.

What God requires of His people may be received by them as an obligation or duty for a variety of reasons. For example a duty may come to them as an imposition, as something that they did not choose or initiate for themselves. Initially such a requirement may seem alien or foreign, out of accord with their own needs and desires. Another reason is that a Christian may be required to do certain actions which are to his own personal disadvantage in the short term. They may cause short-term (or even longer-term) inconvenience, physical and emotional effort, tiredness, the disruption of expectations, and so on. But whether or not something is an obligation which a person has towards God does not depend upon whether the person *feels* an obligation, but on whether there actually *is* an obligation from God. A person may have all sorts of hang-ups, and he may mistakenly regard these as indications of God's will, as obligations to God which in fact are not obligations because there is nothing about them which corresponds to what God actually requires of him as this is revealed in Scripture. Alternatively a person may be careless and carefree and as a result he may come to think that he has no obligations to God at all. So what matters is not what a person feels, whether he feels liberated or constricted in his spirit, but what his actual duties are.

In the previous chapter we saw that the Christian's obligations which give character to his freedom in Christ are embodied in the law of God, the 'moral law' as it is sometimes called. A Christian's freedom in Christ is not an excuse for malice or licence (*1 Pet. 2:16*). Now, more specifically, we can see that the obligations extend to daily work, to 'a lawful calling and diligence in it' as the Westminster Larger Catechism expresses it. A person may have an obligation to do uncongenial work or work for which he thinks that he is personally unfitted. This was presumably so in the case of the Christian slaves of Corinth. And even if a person is in a job that he thinks he is fitted for, which gives him personal satisfaction and a sense of fulfilment, his obligations do not disappear. He has the duty to do the best that he can in the job, the best work with the skills and opportunities which he has. He has the obligation not merely to earn a wage or salary but to do well in the job itself, to become as experienced or skilful or knowledgeable as it is possible to be.

'SECULAR' AND 'CHRISTIAN'

It was noted earlier that it is a misunderstanding of what Paul and John are saying to suppose that their contrast between 'flesh' and 'spirit' is a contrast between body and soul, or between the natural and the spiritual, or the sacred and the secular. The contrast between flesh and spirit cannot be equivalent to the contrast between body and soul because, according to Scripture, God created both of them 'good' (*Gen. 1:31*) and the fall has affected both (*Rom. 3:10–18, Eph. 2:3*). Sin is not to be explained solely by the bodily senses taking over the mind and dominating it, but also by the mind taking a debased direction in such a way that all that a person does serves the creature rather than the Creator. Sin has not split mankind into body (sinful) and soul (sinless). It has resulted in the misdirection of the whole person.

The idea that the daily work of a factory inspector, say, or a librarian is 'secular' and not 'spiritual' or 'Christian' is therefore to be repudiated as being unbiblical. Those who value the insights of the Reformation into the meaning of Scripture should, in particular, wish to repudiate it. Whether such work is spiritual or not depends not only, or chiefly, on the sort of work it is, but on several other matters, and it is on these others matters that emphasis ought to be laid. There is the question of whether the work is lawful, in conformity to God's moral law. Does doing a particular job involve a person in sin? Does it, for example, involve extortion, or the break-up of family life, or the provision of goods and services whose chief or only known purpose is sinful? Taking all factors into account, does the job make the best use of the gifts and opportunities that a person has, equal stress being placed upon both *gift* and *opportunity*? This is a case of 'let every man be fully persuaded in his own mind'. It is a matter of weighing up all factors, taking all reasonable advice and acting accordingly.

Lastly, a Christian must strive to conduct himself in his job in a consistently Christian fashion, both as regards behaviour and (where it is relevant) belief. It is here that a Christian who has work which requires him to take a view of some aspect of life about which Scripture definitely speaks has a double responsibility, for he not only must behave as a Christian, but also he must think biblically in his job, asking whether what he communicates or supports is consistently Christian in its content. But this is not all. As the prevailing motive for all that he does the Christian will have gratitude to God for what He has done for him in Christ, and a concern for God's glory. When Augustine referred to the morality of the pagan word as embodying 'splendid vices' he had this last issue in mind, that while much conduct in society conforms outwardly to biblical standards (for if it did not, then *society* would hardly be possible) it proceeds from pagan rather than from Christian motives and aims.

WORK, UNEMPLOYMENT AND LEISURE

This chapter began by focussing attention on daily work from the perspective of a person's total situation, that arrangement of people and circumstances in which he finds himself. And this calling has in turn been understood in terms of the Christian's call to freedom, and most basically of all in terms of his effectual call by God's grace in Christ. We are now in a position to address the vexed and pressing question of unemployment, and also the Christian's use of the increasing amounts of leisure time which modern industrial society has made possible.

Though the work for which a person gets paid is important, it is a mistake to *identify* a Christian's daily calling with this work and to suppose that a person's calling *is* his work and nothing more. As we have stressed, the New Testament idea of calling is wider than this. It takes in family relationships, social position and religious background, to look no further. All Christians are called to follow Christ even if this involves the patient enduring of acts of injustice which have occurred *because* a person is a Christian (*1 Peter 2: 19–20*). Of course work is important. It requires time and effort, training and expense, it is necessary in order to provide an income, and it would be absurd to suppose that a Christian ought to neglect paid employment.

But as it is a mistake to identify a Christian's calling with his work, for it is wider than his work, so it is a mistake to identify work with paid employment. A person who stops receiving an income from working, either because he is made redundant or because he leaves school and fails to get a job, or because he retires or has enough money to make paid employment unnecessary, does not thereby cease either to work or to have a calling. His calling, with work occupying a large part of it, exists simply in virtue of the fact that he is a Christian. A person does not cease to be a Christian when he retires, or is unemployed, or inherits a fortune.

If these facts are kept in mind it is possible to see how a

Christian ought to regard the fact that he may, for one of a variety of reasons, not have a paid job. Such changes are important shifts in that person's circumstances, and they impose new demands and give rise to new opportunities. Perhaps an unemployed husband will have to look after the home for a time while his wife goes out to work. From a Scriptural point of view, such an arrangement is undesirable, though it is easy to be rash and dogmatic on such a question. Yet it is clear that such an arrangement does not involve sin, and it is perhaps the best way of safeguarding family unity in a far-from-ideal situation. In a sense it is 'the lesser evil', something thrust upon a Christian family by circumstances which are not of its choosing, and is not be be confused with the idea that the wife ought to be the permanent breadwinner.

An unemployed young Christian has ample enforced leisure time. What is he to do? Is he to treat each day and each week as a long holiday? Not only is idleness of this kind psychologically and often physically destructive, it is incompatible with a Christian's calling. While it is not possible or desirable to go into detail over what a Christian ought to do in such circumstances, nevertheless a young person who is unemployed through no fault of his own should not worry or complain himself into inactivity. Are there opportunities to be retrained? Could he secure odd jobs? Ought he to look for work away from home? Does he have a hobby that he can develop?

Paradoxically, while some people become unemployed others in work enjoy greater periods of leisure. The non-Christian attitude is to see leisure in sharp contrast to work, as a period of complete inactivity and self-indulgence. How should the Christian regard it? This question will be difficult to answer if an attempt is made to provide a biblical justification for leisure and recreation by appealing to isolated texts and passages of Scripture which refer, for instance, to Sabbath rest, or to what Ecclesiastes says about the importance of the present, or the Song of Solomon's celebration of love between the sexes. The problem with all such appeals is that they are *forced*, for such passages have no reference to the twentieth-century idea of leisure time and how it may be spent. Either we ought to agree that the Bible has nothing whatsoever to say on this question, or to try to employ a distinctively biblical method of thinking, a method which uses the idea of a person's calling in the wider sense and which also makes calling in this sense intelligible by appealing, beyond it, to God's effectual call by grace.

So how *does* leisure relate to these ideas of calling? Perhaps in the following way. The idea of calling invites each individual to see his life as a whole, before God, and to recognise the obvious fact that people differ from one another. Nothing should be done, in the name of a 'Christian theology of leisure', or of anything else, to erode these differences. For many in the twentieth-century, in the West, the enjoyment of leisure time which is not wholly occupied with recovering from the effects of working is a fact that can be taken for granted. It is one of the 'inputs' into our lives, it represents a new set of opportunities along with, say, the higher standards of provision for health that we have all come to expect. And since 'calling' is not equivalent to 'paid work', increasing amounts of leisure ought not to be an embarrassment to the Christian any more than the fact that small-pox has been eliminated should embarrass him. Formerly life consisted in working and resting from work. Now it consists in working, resting and 'leisure time'.

But 'leisure' is a word for many different things, playing sport and watching it, travelling, developing sophisticated hobbies, and so on. If the differences between people which we have been stressing as part of the biblical account of 'calling' and the different kinds of leisure are added together then very many different attitudes both to paid work and to leisure and to their relation are possible. Some people find fulfilment in one life-long, week-long job, some in a combination of work and leisure, some in work which is not employment, some in work which is play for others, and so forth. All such differences are compatible with Christian integrity and with the idea of each Christian having a calling. What is not compatible with this is any activity which is sinful, or for which the motive and end is unchristian, or which is the imposition of one pattern of living by others. Again, 'let every man be fully persuaded in his own mind'.

The view that there is a theology of play or leisure which could prescribe amounts and kinds of leisure for everyone is absurd, however well-intentioned it may be. But it is also threatening, threatening to Christian liberty and to the development of the individual Christian's calling before God. Not all Christian activities need justification in other terms. For part of a Christian's calling, as we have seen, is where possible to develop an intrinsic interest in his paid work, something worthwhile in its own terms. And if this is true of paid work, how much more is it true of unpaid work and leisure. In them the Christian is free to enjoy aspects of God's creation for their own sake.

6: *Boundaries and Limits*

We have tried to show that one way for the Christian to avoid split-mindedness is to think of his life as a calling. In the first place it is a life brought into being by God's effectual call. It is a call to freedom, freedom from the Old Testament ceremonial law, and freedom to serve God in obedience to Him, a freedom made possible by the indwelling of the Holy Spirit and by his renewing work. And it is a call which reaches to the whole of a person's life-situation, in all its detail. Such a life – in principle – knows no splits between the 'sacred' and the 'secular', or between 'the body' and 'the spirit', or between 'religious truth' and 'scientific truth', but is dedicated to the unifying of these areas of conflict in one integrated life, a life to which each Christian is called.

In sketching this view in broad outline much detail and some necessary qualifications have had to be omitted. This is an appropriate place to glance at some of these qualifications in order to try to put a little more detail into the argument which has been presented, and to 'earth' it in a realistic fashion.

BOUNDED BY THE LAW

God's moral law and Christian freedom when properly understood are no more in conflict than are law and grace. And yet Christian freedom ought not to be thought of in individualistic terms, as if a person can be detached from all others, and live anonymously. The law itself is a reminder that each person lives in a world of other people to some of whom he owes responsibilities. Such responsibilities constrain and direct Christian freedom, but they also discipline and enrich it. This can be illustrated by referring to three areas of responsibility: the Sabbath and Christian worship, the family, and the state.

Earlier it was argued that the New Testament's endorsement of the moral law makes it reasonable to suppose that the New Testament also endorses the principle of the first day's rest in seven even though such a command is nowhere provided in explicit terms. In the apostolic era the one day of rest became the Lord's Day, the first day of the week, the day of Christ's resurrection. If this distinction between six days' work and one day's rest and worship is observed then it at once provides a boundary or a structural element to a Christian's calling. For it is an abiding reminder to the Christian that his daily calling is sustained by the appointed means of grace in the church. Furthermore, however important his daily calling is, and it is important, it is not all-important. His calling, however all-embracing it is, is not bounded by the horizons of this life, but looks forward to the life to come. The day of rest which he enjoys each week is a foretaste of the heavenly rest to which he is hastening. His work at present is marked by sin, weakness and failure. His bodily weakness needs renewing by rest as his sin needs pardoning and removing. Finally the appointed pattern of work and worship reminds the Christian that he has obligations to the church of God on earth.

Family life also structures and limits ties and responsibilities, and this fact receives great prominence in Scripture. The obligations of children to parents, and of parents to children (*Eph. 6:1–4*), of husbands to wives and wives to husbands (*Eph. 5:22–33*) are emphasised. In considering 1 Corinthians 7 it has been seen that, according to Paul's teaching, as far as possible marriages are not to be split up by the gospel, but the Christian partner (in those marriages where the other partner is not a Christian) is so to foster the relationship that, under God, the partner may also be converted. A Christian is to provide for his own house (*1 Tim. 5:8*).

However such responsibilities are expressed in detail, their existence is a forceful reminder that the Christian's calling is not individualistic. Each of us is not simply a unit, an atom, living in self-sufficiency. Relationships with other people are not a matter of casual choice, living with people and separating from them as we see fit. Some of the deepest relationships are not chosen at all. None of us has chosen to be in the families to which we belong, and yet these family bonds give rise to deep affections and loyalties. The Bible also emphasises throughout its pages that the family is the vehicle through which God's grace comes to the individuals within it, not in a purely biological fashion, but through nurture, teaching and example (*2 Tim. 1:5*) in accordance with God's promise.

In the period of time between Moses and Christ the nation-state of Israel and the church of God were virtually co-terminous, being ruled by one Lord through laws and ordinances which covered not only worship but most aspects of the nation's political and social life, and did so in great detail. In the New Testament God's saving grace becomes 'internationalised'. It is not confined to one nation or race, but men and women of any and all nations are called by grace. The barrier between Jew and Gentile is broken in Christ (*Eph. 2:14*). God does not rule any nation in the manner in which He ruled the Jewish nation. But the consequence of this is not that the Christian is not to care about or to ignore the nation in which he resides and the government under which he lives. The Christian church is not to be a secret society, like the Masons or the Mafia, with rules of its own which override those of the state. Nor is it to 'free ride', making use of the many advantages of stable government but contributing nothing towards it. Quite the opposite. The New Testament provides explicit recognition of the state as a distinct social unity which has a central political authority with the power to legislate and to raise taxes, and even to take life, a state which is to receive the obedience and honour of Christians (*1 Pet. 2:13–15*) and to be the subject of their prayers (*1 Tim. 2:1–3*). So not only does the Christian have allegiances to the church and to his family, he has obligations to the state and ties to the nation in which he is born or domiciled.

The New Testament does not offer a political theory but it places stress on Christian practice, on the actual situations which confronted the early Christian church. And its emphasis is upon the need for obedience to the laws of the state. For the state is ordained by God (*Rom. 13:1*), and there are great advantages both to the individual Christian and the church from a social and political situation that is stable. It is by quiet, peaceable and loyal citizenship that the Christian is to be known. He is to wield such influence as he may have, not by attempting to overturn the state or to promote radical reform in the name of Christ, but through personal influence and example within the system. As was shown earlier there is no suggestion in the New Testament, in either the teaching of Christ or the apostles, that the Christian may take part in movements of radical social and political change, much less in revolution. It may be that there are situations in which there is such desperate general lawlessness, or tyranny in government, that the very idea of law-abidingness becomes impossible. A deep-seated wholesale change may be called for to which the Christian may give his support. But such situations are not to be sought or engineered, and should only be a last resort.

But what is to be done where the state enacts laws which would oblige the Christian to sin? It is plain that in such circumstances the Christian ought to obey God rather than men (*Acts 5:29*). He cannot be passively obedient in such a situation, claiming that the voice of the government is the voice of God. So the Christian is to render to Caesar what is Caesar's and to Christ what is Christ's (*Matt. 22:21*). This is not to adopt a temporising or fence-sitting policy, if the claims of many political leaders throughout history to be entitled to the absolute allegiance of their citizens is borne in mind.

Yet even here it is important to exercise great care, for while the New Testament implies that civil disobedience is necessary when the alternative is sin, it nowhere suggests that civil disobedience is necessary, or even permitted, when the state enacts laws which *allow* sin. The distinction between laws which require sin, and laws which permit it, is a crucial one. No doubt the taxes which were collected from the Christians in New Testament times would be used for some purposes of which the Christians would disapprove. But this fact was not regarded by the apostles as a sufficient reason for acts of civil disobedience.

The Lord's day and the church, the family and the state together impart a structure and a shape to the Christian's calling, a shape which the New Testament explicitly sanctions. It is within such a shape that Christian culture is to be pursued and, with the divine blessing, to flourish. Such arrangements are not to be thought of as an imposition but as a setting within which a Christian can feel 'at home' and within which his calling may be exercised and bear fruit as his various gifts and graces are developed.

But there are problems, in two main areas. The first problem is the familiar difficulty when one set of obligations and loyalties encroaches upon another. The limits to a Christian's loyalty to the state have already been noted. But there are other possible clashes of loyalty, between family life and daily work, between the demands of work and of the church, and so on. And there is the whole question of whether Christian standards may be expected of people who are not Christians, and of the extent to which a Christian should attempt to impose such standards upon others. Here it is not merely a matter of whether and to what extent such influence should be exerted upon others, but also of recognising the fact that there is rarely a vacuum of influence in society. Often the choice is between supporting trends which are consistent with and supportive of the Christian faith and trends which are definitely hostile. We need look no further than laws affecting marriage and the family for examples of such conflicts.

CALLING AND COMPROMISE

We should not therefore be surprised that there are acute practical problems for the Christian who conscientiously pursues his daily calling. They are problems involving a conflict of loyalties and the ordering of priorities. Behind these looms the spectre of compromise. How far should a Christian make concessions in a situation in which he cannot expect to get all his own way?

For the faithful Christian 'compromise' is an ugly word. He remembers the teaching of Paul about 'another gospel' in Galatians 1, and Christ's warning that it is impossible to serve God and Mammon (*Matt. 6:24*). The idea of tampering with God's truth, the truth 'once delivered to the saints' (*Jude 3*), is abhorrent to him, as is the idea of compromising over standards. Because of this abhorrence of compromise it is easy to suppose that the Christian can find no room for yielding at any level. But it is necessary to see that there is a certain sort of flexibility that is both inevitable and acceptable to the Christian. This comes about when he is not concerned with upholding the divinely revealed deposit of faith, nor with being made to sin, but with the practical question of finding his way through the competing obligations which come to him inescapably. The Christian, like every one else, has limited time and energy and personal influence. How ought he to use these gifts?

Within the framework sketched earlier there is a wide latitude, and there is a world of difference between a situation which has to be accepted because it is the best that can be achieved in the circumstances and one which represents the best possible outcome, the best in all the circumstances. For each person the best possible situation seems to be, quite naturally, one in which he gets his own way. But how many situations are there in which this is possible? Even a dictator is constrained a good deal by what other people are willing to do. He needs their active co-operation. And for anyone else, to do precisely what he wants to do is only possible with relatively trivial matters. There is need to co-operate with others and to make concessions at every turn. 'Getting one's own way' is more a mark of childishness than of maturity.

One reason for the failure to recognise this is the desire to make every decision a matter of principle and therefore non-negotiable. But to suppose that everything is a matter of principle is an unworkable absurdity. What *is* a matter of principle for the Christian is the integrity of the gospel, the confessing of the faith, and the need not to be made to sin and not to make other people sin. Within these limits meeting other people half way is not only possible but essential if human society is to persist at all, and if the Christian is to form a part of it.

What light does Scripture throw on these matters? It teaches, to begin with, that for the Christian there is a range of actions which is 'indifferent', which God neither commands nor forbids, but which a Christian is free to perform or to refrain from performing as he sees fit (*Rom. 14*). Because of the possibility that points of view will clash the New Testament calls upon the Christian to exercise forbearance (*Eph. 4:2, Col. 3:13*) and as far as possible to live at peace with everyone (*Rom. 12:18*). However important forbearance and peace are within the setting of the church, in fact the New Testament does not make a sharp distinction between what ought to happen inside the church and what outside. It does not advocate two different ethical standards. The Christian is to do good, not only to the 'household of faith' but more generally (*Gal. 6:10*). And in a striking phrase, one which he normally reserves for the relationship of Christians in the church, Paul refers to all people, Christian and non-Christian alike, as being 'members one of another' (*Eph. 4:25*).

As the calling of a Christian is a calling to live one life, a life which is not to be artifically broken up into 'Christian' and 'non-Christian' segments, so his behaviour ought not to be in accordance with two different standards, one for the church and one outside it, except that within the church there may be expected to be stronger ties of unity and affection. But to imagine that a person could be a saint in the church and a 'man of the world' outside it is to support a hypocrisy which the Bible consistently condemns (*Matt. 23:28*).

And so if there is to be forbearance in the church there ought also to be forbearance in those relationships outside the church in which a Christian is inevitably involved.

There ought to be a spirit of meekness, a willingness to get on with people. It is to such situations that the Saviour's often misquoted and misunderstood words about passivity and the turning of the other cheek (*Matt. 5:39*) apply, situations in which a Christian can compromise without sin and without a failure of duty on his part. Christ says that if one is called upon to yield to others in such situations then one must.

There are a number of possible reasons why Christians may deny that such compromise is necessary in fulfilling their callings in the wider sense. As we have seen a person may think that the whole of his life is as inviolable as the gospel itself. He may think that since compromise over the truth of the gospel is out of the question, compromise over other matters is also out of the question. But there are other influences to be considered.

The thought of compromise suggests to some that the compromiser is doing evil in order that good may result, something which the Bible condemns (*Rom. 3:8*). But this need not be so, and the thought that it must be so is based upon a confusion. To do evil that good may come is to do something which is sinful with the hope or expectation that some benefit will result. But compromise need not involve this, for there are situations in which the Christian must be willing to cooperate with others *in a way which does not require him to sin*, or others to sin. It is plain confusion to suppose that what is, from the Christian's own standpoint, less than ideal, is positively evil, and that a Christian who has to settle for less than the best is sinning.

If I am a member of a committee charged with deciding what colour the office walls are to be painted, and I think that green would be the ideal colour, while everyone else prefers white, I am not sinning if I agree to white. And there are less trivial cases also, where I may judge that it is better to continue to be a member of the committee, even if decisions go against me, than to resign at the first opportunity. Besides there is a world of difference between a situation in which a person initiates action which is sinful in order that good may come, and a situation which is not of the person's making but in which he is forced to make a choice between two alternatives, neither of which is ideal.

There is a further influence which tends to make us think that compromise of any kind is an evil, a confusion about the limits of a person's responsibility. Each of us is responsible to God for himself, for those for whom we have responsibility and for anyone else who is in obvious need and whom we are in a position to help. But we are not responsible for everyone else, and for every decision taken by them.

Suppose that I am employed as a plumber and required by my boss to repair the plumbing in a Bingo Hall. I might not care for Bingo, and I may even think that besides being a waste of time it is positively sinful. Should I repair the leak, or refuse to do so and risk dismissal? Mending a pipe in a Bingo Hall is not sinful. But would I not be 'aiding and abetting' the playing of Bingo? In a way I am, of course. Perhaps I also am if I do not do everything in my power to get the Bingo Hall closed down. But my responsibility as a plumber, where I am not being called upon to sin, is to my employer, and the responsibility for taking on the work is *his* responsibility. But in saying this, am I not shuffling off all responsibility? Not at all. For I am responsible for doing a good job on the pipe and I am certainly responsible if I do what is sinful. The SS officers who operated the gas-chambers could not avoid responsibility for their actions by laying it on to their superiors, because their action was horrifyingly sinful whether done under orders or not.

The fact that a Christian lives in a community of people limits his responsibility even though the exact boundaries of that responsibility are sometimes hard to discern. But think of what the world would be like if responsibility were not limited. The postman would have to open all the mail to see whether or not he approved of what he was carrying, the taxi-driver would have to cross-examine his fares. It would be impossible to work for a firm whose products might be used in the course of sin, or to buy goods from people who might use the profits they make in ways which are sinful. The fact that other people are responsible means that one person cannot be totally responsible for all the actual consequences of an action which he has performed. Otherwise life would be unlivable, for then such a person could only contribute to a situation for which he took total responsibility and in which he was able to force or manipulate others. The alternative would be total withdrawal from society. Happily such drastic reactions are not required of us. The Christian is called to do the best that he can in the total situation of which he forms a part. This requires him to cooperate with others where this does not lead him to commit sin, or where his actions do not require others to sin.

CHRISTIAN FREEDOM AND INDIFFERENCE

Earlier we glanced at the teaching of the New Testament in which there are certain actions which are neither commanded by God nor forbidden by Him, but are 'indifferent'. It is worth exploring this idea a little further. To do what is forbidden by God is to transgress positively, and not to do what is commanded is to commit iniquity negatively. But to do or not to do what is indifferent, what is neither forbidden nor commanded, is neither iniquity nor transgression.

The fact that there are significant areas of human conduct in which actions are neither commanded by God nor forbidden by Him is an important characteristic of Christian ethics, and it marks it off from another very influential type of thinking about ethics, namely utilitarianism. According to utilitarianism, a person ought to live in such a way as to maximise total human satisfaction. Since every action, no matter how personal or trivial, may make a contribution to the sum-total of human happiness, it follows that a conscientious and consistent utilitarian will live his life on a treadmill. For every action is such that either he ought to do it (because it will contribute to total human happiness) or he ought not (because it will not). There is no escape, because from the utilitarian standpoint there are no actions which are 'indifferent'. But in Christian ethics there is what is commanded and what is forbidden and, besides these, what is neither commanded nor forbidden.

The conduct which is neither commanded nor forbidden is sometimes referred to as the area of 'Christian liberty'. This phrase is misleading, however, if it suggests that Christian liberty is *not* experienced by the Christian as he does what God commands. For as we saw earlier the whole of a Christian's life, insofar as it is marked by the keeping of God's law out of gratitude to God for His mercy, is a life of liberty. Such a life is freedom lived in the service of God. In such a life the Christian 'comes to himself', he begins to live in accordance with his true nature, a nature made in God's image. So the whole of a Christian's life insofar as it is lived consistently is a life of liberty.

It is also misleading to call conduct which is neither commanded nor forbidden 'Christian liberty', because the phrase may suggest that in such areas of life, concerning actions which are neither commanded nor forbidden, God is not involved. But, of course, this is not so. God is involved in every detail of life, even of those areas which He has neither commanded nor forbidden, and He is to be served in these matters as well.

Paul makes this clear in the classic treatment of the Christian and what is indifferent, as found in Romans 14. He is dealing with those who have scruples about eating certain kinds of meat and observing special days. Paul teaches that in this difference of opinion over what may be eaten, the one who thinks that he is at liberty to eat meat of any kind is 'strong'. Such a person's view is in accordance with the true nature of things as created by God. Those who are vegetarian because they think that this is more in accord with God's will are 'weak', for they mistakenly think that God has forbidden certain kinds of eating. And yet, Paul adds, this difference is not to become a matter of disputation among Christians, any more than is a difference of opinion over the keeping of certain 'special' days, but everyone is to be fully persuaded in his own mind (*v.5*). It is perfectly permissible to be a vegetarian, and to keep special days, provided that one does not attempt to make such practices a matter of Christian obligation. If such an attempt is made then the liberty of other Christians is compromised.

Paul stresses three times that Christian conduct about such matters is 'unto the Lord' (*v.6*). Each Christian, whatever his judgment about such practices turns out to be, forms that judgment in the Lord's sight and as a person who is accountable only to the Lord. Even in these affairs Christ is served. The fact that such differences are permissible does not imply that a person is not accountable.

Why does Paul call one group 'the strong' and the other 'the weak'? Although these terms refer to differences which are allowable, nevertheless Paul implies that 'the strong' adopt the correct view while 'the weak' are mistaken. It is frequently said that 'the strong' have a responsibility not to offend 'the weak' in the sense that they are not to do anything that would upset them or to cause comment. But this view, though widespread, is based upon a misunderstanding of what Paul means by 'offend', which is strongly connected with the idea of personal responsibility before God. A stumbling-block or an occasion to fall is not merely something that causes a person to be upset, but which causes him to sin, to violate his own conscience by doing things which, at present, his conscience forbids. John Murray, commenting on Romans 14:13, says

> Here these terms are used metaphorically and convey the same thought, namely, that which becomes the occasion of falling into sin. In the most aggravated sense an occasion of falling is placed before a person when the intention is that of seduction; there is deliberate intent that the person may fall. We are not to suppose that the strong in this case are conceived of as actuated by that express intent. But this only accentuates the care that must be taken by the strong in the circumstance of weakness on the side of their brethren. The strong are regarded as placing a stumblingblock when they do not desist from what becomes an occasion of stumbling for the weak brother.

So, according to John Murray, to cause to stumble is to cause to sin, to be an occasion of sin. And to be an occasion of sin, in this situation, is to bring it about, through inconsiderateness, that a person acts against his conscience, against his better judgment, doing something which he believes, albeit mistakenly, God has forbidden. This fact is clearly brought out in verses 14 and 22, where Paul indicates that 'uncleanness' in eating is a matter of the individual conscience, and that a person who acts against his conscience is 'damned', that is, judged or condemned.

Summarising, three themes stand out in Paul's discussion in Romans 14. There is, to begin with, an area of conduct where there is no express command from God, where a person must form his own judgment regarding the rights and wrongs of the situation. Then Paul says that in such a situation a person is not so to act as to cause another person to sin by making him violate the judgment of his own conscience about how he ought to behave. Rather than allow this to happen a person is to forbear doing what, for him as a 'strong' person, it would be perfectly permissible to do, for example, to eat certain kinds of meat. Finally, for Paul the individual conscience, and the individual's responsibility to God, are paramount. To cause another person to stumble is to 'set him at nought', to 'destroy' him, and to forget that each person must give account of himself to God (*v. 14*).

So Paul's teaching underscores what we concluded earlier, that the Christian should not put himself into any situation in which he is made to sin, or in which he makes others to sin. But within these limits co-operation and compromise, in the local church and in a person's wider calling, are both possible and necessary.

RIGHTS AND DUTIES

We are arguing that a person's effectual call by God's grace and his 'calling' in the wider and more general sense are intertwined. The Christian lives one life, a life which is given sense and direction by his call by grace. His wider calling must never be allowed to swallow up or take the place of God's effectual call through the gospel. And Scripture attaches considerable importance to 'staying put' in one's calling, and even of patiently enduring unjust suffering. The Christian may, in pursuit of his calling, have to forbear and compromise, so long as he and others are not caused to sin by such conduct.

It may be objected that such an account of the Christian in society is too passive. Why, it may be asked, is such emphasis put on the providence of God in a person's calling, on enduring injustice, and on the need to compromise and cooperate. Has the Christian no rights in society? Is he not able to assert himself in the name of Christ and to attempt to overcome manifest injustice and oppression? Such a question is all the more pressing at a time when people are demanding their 'rights', when the list of such rights grows longer by the hour, and when many attempt to secure such rights for others in the name of Christ by 'liberating' them from 'oppressive structures'. Does the Christian have no rights? And is it not a part of his calling to assert such rights both on his own behalf and on the behalf of others?

In 1 Peter 2, Peter shows the need for Christian slaves to be obedient to their masters, even to those masters who are awkward and unfair. He does not advise that the Christian slave is to agitate, or to refuse to co-operate, or to run away. Nor does he recommend that the slave ought to think of himself as part of a spiritual élite to which the ordinary duties and ties of life do not apply. Rather the Christian slave is 'called' (*v. 21*) to follow Christ in patiently enduring wrongful treatment, for did not Christ his Saviour endure such treatment in going to the cross for his redemption? And is the disciple to be above his Lord? Quite clearly Peter's words apply not only to Christian slaves, an extreme case, but to every Christian in society. Each Christian is called upon to be a Christ-follower, not in seeking martyrdom but in patient suffering because he is a Christian when divine providence places such suffering in his path.

At the same time the positive implications of the principle that the Christian, however submissive he must be, ought not to sin or to make others to sin must not be underestimated. Using the language of rights it could be said that Scripture teaches that each person has a God-given right not to sin or to cause others to sin. And bearing in mind the extent of the duties which the law of God requires a person to fulfil, such rights are not insignificant. For example, a parent has a God-given obligation to his children to provide for them and to bring them up in accordance with biblical standards. If the parent has such a God-given obligation then he also has a God-given right to take proper steps to secure this particular end. He may legitimately act to secure such rights if they are denied to him, though here, as more generally, a Christian parent will not wish to act hastily and he must always balance the advantages and disadvantages of any situation.

The implications of such duties and rights are far-reaching, though one set of duties and rights has to be balanced against another. This is one reason, incidentally, why the Christian has to be wary of what is sometimes called 'one issue' politics. Life does not consist of one issue, about housing, say, or abortion, but of many complex and interlocking issues. And while the Christian may have strongly-held beliefs about one issue, because he regards it as involving sin, he will hesitate to man the barricades to get it altered at all costs, because he also values and has obligations for maintaining general habits of law-abidingness.

Besides the right not to sin or to cause others to sin, does the Christian also have the right to *prevent* others sinning? This is an extremely difficult area. A Christian is to love his neighbour as himself. He will attempt to prevent a person obviously harming himself or suffering harm. He will do what he can to rescue someone from icy water or to prevent a parked car from rolling backwards to destruction. He will try to gain political and legal backing to support the duties which he has in the family, the church and society at large. But does the Christian have a duty to stop others from doing wrong when such wrong-doing does not cause him to sin? Attractive as the policy of 'live and let live' may seem, it is often not possible to carry it out. This is partly because modern society is so interlocked, and partly for the reason that if biblical standards are not maintained then anti-biblical standards gain momentum. Live and let live is an attractive and realistic option for the Christian but only if every one else lives and lets live. But in practice people at large do not act in this way.

Is there anything more to be said? As noted earlier, the Acts of the Apostles records the triumphant progress of the gospel from its early beginnings in Jerusalem to its penetration to the heart of the Roman Empire. This progress is pivoted upon the fact that Paul was a Roman citizen, and that he was prepared to exercise the rights attached to this status, the right not to be beaten without a trial (*Acts 16:37*) and to appeal to Caesar (*Acts 25:11*) for trial. His appeal took him to Rome, under imperial escort. And the fact of Paul's assertion of his Roman citizenship cannot be an accident. Is it included in Scripture to teach Christians about their rights? Is it not in striking contrast, even contradiction, to the teaching of Peter about the need for slaves to be submissive? Does the New Testament offer two conflicting attitudes, that of Paul the Roman citizen and that of Peter the adviser to Christian slaves?

There is a distinction to be drawn between two kinds of rights. Some rights are basic and God-given, the rights which all men have not to be made to sin and the corresponding duty not to cause others to sin. There are other particular rights which have grown up as a result of legislation. In England the law conveys rights to citizens over and above the basic rights which every Christian must claim. For example, a person may have the right to have his children educated at the expense of the state, or the right to receive free medical attention or redundancy pay. Following Paul's example a Christian can make use of such rights with a good conscience. And yet such rights are not to be confused with his basic right that he is not to be made to sin. This can be seen from the fact that the same legal authority which gives a person, under certain circumstances, the right to accept a state pension, also gives him the right to commit adultery. Many of the rights which citizens have are the result of legislation which permits sin. And so they cannot be identical in character with the basic right which all have not to be made to sin.

Given such legal rights it is open to the Christian to make use of them, as Paul did. He must ask, Is the action conferred by such a right sinful? If it is not sinful, and would not cause others to sin, would claiming the right be a useful thing to do in these circumstances? Would it bring more harm than good? It is surely in this spirit that Paul insisted on his rights as a Roman citizen. It was not that Paul was impressed by the fact that he had certain basic rights that he could insist upon, but that the Roman law gave him rights which he judged that it would be wise to exercise to further the work of the kingdom of God. There may be other occasions when it is judged correct *not* to exercise one's legal rights in this way.

The question is sometimes raised whether the first priority should be individual salvation or social action. But there cannot really be any doubt what the answer should be. For to be authentically Christian any activity in society, whether it takes the form of upholding the rights of others not to be made to sin and to suffer, or of entrepreneurship and risk-taking in business, must be an

outworking of a Christian's call, the effect of regenerating grace. And social action or business activity,
besides being undertaken in a lawful manner, must also
not undermine the structure of biblical law regarding
the worship of the true God, family life and private
property.

CONCLUSION

As the Christian attempts to carry out his wider calling,
questions about the structure of that calling, and of its
boundaries, naturally arise. In this chapter an attempt
has been made to acknowledge the existence of these
questions, and to offer the beginning of answers to them,
answers which, it is believed, are in accordance with
Scripture. But such questions can be complex, and both
the ordinary Christian and the Christian pastor must be
prepared to think hard and long about how the unchan-
ging truth of Scripture applies to the changing circumstances of life. Complexity is unavoidable if Christians are to think realistically about their calling in the
midst of the practicalities of everyday life. For while the
Christian is not *of* the world he is *in* the world, and many
complex and competing demands call for decision. To
put off decision is often to have the decision made for one
by the ongoing sweep of circumstances.

The purpose of this chapter has been to provide
something of the flavour of Christian thinking and
attitudes in everyday life and so to avoid the criticism
that the idea of the Christian's calling in daily life is
nothing but a pious platitude. On the contrary it is a
calling to a serious and distinctive 'life-style'. But that
life-style does not come automatically, or by a few
superficial changes and the adopting of slogans. It is a
manner of life that can only be sustained through a

continuous process of thinking about how the faith relates to new issues, and to old issues in new guises.

Perhaps some will say that the discussion has not been detailed enough. But there is a good reason for keeping the discussion brief, quite apart from the virtue of brevity, for the very essence of the Christian's calling is that he is effectively called by divine grace in a situation which is not of his making but which is God's call to him. He is given principles and examples in Scripture in terms of which he is to think and which he must apply to the particularities of his own situation. Each Christian is responsible for the detailed applications of these biblical principles to his own life. To his own Master he stands or falls. Each one of us must given account of *himself* to God.

7: Calling and Consummation

Although he is destined for another world the believer's first responsibility lies in this world. He is united to Christ and already has eternal life (*John 6:54*). He is seated in the heavenly places in Christ (*Eph. 2:6*). And yet he remains in this world, with all its awkwardnesses, frustrations and temptations, as well as its challenges and joys. This world is the theatre of the Christian's calling. And yet Scripture also teaches that this world is fading. The 'outward man' is decaying day by day and the matters which are eternal, which are of abiding importance, are hidden from view (*2 Cor. 4:18*). It is the mark of the worldly man that he is totally absorbed in and captivated by what is 'seen' and 'present' (*Luke 12:13–21*).

How can these important strands of biblical teaching, which seem to be in conflict, be brought into harmony? How can a Christian be concerned at one and the same time about his daily calling in this life and the unseen reality of the world to come? One way in which some harmony is gained is by stressing that this present world is an arena of spiritual discipline. The temptations and infirmities of life are intended by the Lord to produce Christian virtue in the believer. The New Testament certainly teaches this (*2 Cor. 4:17*). The Christian needs to be taught the lesson that God's grace is sufficient (*2 Cor. 12:9*) and he needs to acquire the virtues of patience, experience and brotherly kindness (*2 Peter 1:5–7*).

Such virtues could hardly be gained or manifested in a world that was totally free from hardship and need.

Does the scriptural idea of this world as a 'vale of tears' provide the *only* link between this world and the next? Does it exhaust what Scripture means by the Christian's 'heavenly calling' (*Heb. 3:1, 2 Thess. 1:11*)? If so, does this not neutralise all that has so far been said about the Christian's calling in this life? Many Christians do effectively neutralise it, so that to them this world is the place of spiritual warfare and nothing more. It is a world to be shunned, to be fled from. Insofar as by 'the world' is meant all that is organised in neglect of or in opposition to God, 'the world' of 1 John 2:17, then the world is indeed not to be loved or served. But if by 'the world' is meant the whole of the Lord's providential orderings as they affect the individual Christian, then it is an impossibility to flee from the world. One might as soon think that one can flee from the Lord Himself.

If the believer is not to love the world or its 'things' (*1 John 2:15*), then how are his present opportunities and responsibilities to be linked to the life to come? What is the positive relationship between the Christian's present calling and his heavenly calling?

In an attempt to answer this a start will be made at what may seem to be an unusual place. In order to fulfil His divine 'calling' the eternal Son of God took human nature. Not a human body merely, but human nature. Where is the human nature of the Son of God now? The biblical answer, in brief, is that Jesus Christ remains for ever both God and man. 'Two whole, perfect and distinct natures, the Godhead and the manhood, were inseparably joined together in one person, without conversion, composition, or confusion' (Westminster Confession of Faith, VIII.2). God and man having come together in Jesus Christ, they are never more to be separated. The eternal Son of God is for ever the God-man. He is a priest for ever after the order of Melchisedec (*Heb. 6:20*).

What is the importance of this amazing and mysterious fact for the Christian's daily calling? The connection may not seem to be obvious, but it is a reminder of two important truths. One is that there is a palpable, physical 'carry-over' from this present world to the world to come. However difficult it is to grasp this fact, and to answer all the questions that come to mind, it is a plain implication of biblical teaching. Whatever the exact transformation that Jesus underwent at His resurrection, His human nature, including His body, with all the relevant psychological and physical properties, remained intact.

So the fact of the resurrection of Christ forbids the thought that there is a dualism between this world and the world to come. The world to come is not a world of purely intellectual ideals, a world of eternal spiritual stillness. It is a world of minds and bodies, at the centre of which is the embodied eternal Son of God.

The second truth that Christ's bodily resurrection and ascension teach is that the world to come will bear traces of this world. It already bears those traces, because the risen Christ is there. The world to come brings to open triumph the finished work of Christ, and the character of the glorified Christ, as regards His human nature, is partly the product of His earthly career. He would not be as He now is in heaven if He had not been as He was on earth. The memory of what He suffered, and the obedience that He 'learned' (*Heb. 5:8*) are carried over into the world to come. It is because of this that the writer of the letter to the Hebrews says that Jesus is able to be a merciful and faithful high priest, one who is sympathetic to the needs of His people (*Heb. 4:15,16*).

The significance of the bodily resurrection of Christ is linked in Scripture to the bodily resurrection of believers.

Because He lives they shall live also. The link is not merely that the one parallels the other but that Christ's resurrection is the reason for and the pledge of the resurrection of believers. The resurrection of Christ not only controls the fact of the believer's resurrection, it also determines its nature. As Christ carries the memories of His momentous conflict into glory, (and the scars of His suffering), so believers take with them the effects of the regenerating and sanctifying work of the Spirit as these have been produced during their life-long callings. It is highly significant that believers are urged to present their *bodies* as living sacrifices (*Rom. 12:1*) and to face a judgment on the basis of what they have done in the *body* (*2 Cor. 5:10*).

So the life-long process of sanctification in the believer is not some ethereal change, another layer of life that is wholly unrelated to daily life. Sanctification is the re-making of a person in the image of God in righteousness and true holiness (*Eph. 4:24*), not a person's spirit only, but the whole of his being.

A man's or a woman's personality develops inseparably from the kind of life that he or she leads. The dispositions and skills, the development of judgment and taste, besides the development of moral virtues and devotional attitudes, are all aspects of sanctification. So that a trained eye and hand, the development of mental powers and skills, as these unfold in the course of a person's life as he or she fulfils the 'calling', are part of the divine re-making which is called sanctification, because they are inextricably intertwined with moral and spiritual renewal. All these are aspects of a person's character that are inseparable from him, just as his memory is inseparable from him. To suppose that the life of eternal bliss in Christ will be a memory-less, skill-less or character-less affair is to do violence to the whole doctrine of sanctification as this is taught in the New Testament.

So whatever heaven will be like in detail, the God-man will be there, the Lamb who has been slain. And His people, who have come out of great tribulation, will be there as well. And as Christ bears the character and the marks of His calling, so will all of His people bear the character and marks of their calling and of the grace of God experienced in them.

The teaching that there is to be a 'carry over' from this world to the world to come is given further support from various other teachings of the New Testament. In the parable of the talents (*Matt. 25,14-30*) Jesus taught that after the judgment the talents of the faithful steward are to be augmented by the talents of which the unfaithful steward is deprived. Whatever exactly such a transfer may mean – and it would be unwise to press the detail – the parable is clearly teaching that possession of the talents (in the case of the faithful steward) is something which persists after the judgment.

In 1 Corinthians 3, Paul teaches that the work of a faithful minister 'abides' (*v. 14*). Paul is writing about the character of the gospel ministry, and about how it is possible to build either a valuable or value-less super-structure on the foundation (*v. 10*), yet it cannot be that Paul's teaching is restricted to ministers alone. For the *principles* to which he is appealing apply to all believers. As is the case with ministers, so all believers have a 'work'. There is to be a judgment of all, ministers and others, at which the worthwhileness of a man's work will be assessed. All believers are to build in accordance with the doctrine of the gospel, not necessarily as ministers of the Word of God but as faithful stewards. It would be absurd to suppose that the principles of 1 Corinthians 3 apply *only* to ministers and not to all believers. If such principles do apply exclusively to ministers, then what *other* principles apply to believers who are not ministers?

Later on in the letter Paul exhorts the believers, in the light of the certainty of their resurrection and of the incorruptible inheritance that awaits them in Christ (*1 Cor. 15:50–58*), to continue to abound in the work of the Lord (*v. 58*). What is this work? Is it restricted only to the work of the ministry? Is it confined to the work of prayer and praise and personal evangelism? No doubt it includes such activities. But what would the phrase mean to the Christian slaves at Corinth whom Paul had urged to remain where they were? What was 'the work of the Lord' to which they were called and which would not be in vain because of Christ's resurrection? Surely Paul is referring here to any work to which a Christian is lawfully called, to any piece of faithful discipleship.

According to Paul's teaching in Colossians Christ created all things, the visible and invisible powers and authorities of the creation (*1:16*). And God the Father reconciled all things, the things in heaven and the things in the earth, to Christ (*1.20*). So besides the human aspect of redemption, the salvation of the church through Christ, there is also a cosmic aspect, according to which the whole creation groans, awaiting the day of redemption (*Rom. 8:19–22*), the day when the new heavens and the new earth are to be established (*2 Pet. 3:13*). As Herman Bavinck expressed it

It is certainly wrong to suppose that the sole purpose of the creation was to produce the fall; on the contrary, by means of God's creative activity, a universe that will remain even in the state of glory was called into being. The fall took place not only in order that there might be a 'creature in the condition of misery', but together with all its consequences it will retain its significance. Christ not merely became a *Mediator*, which would have been all that was necessary for the expiation of sin, but he was also ordained by God to be the *Head* of the church. The history of the universe is not a mere means which loses its value as soon as the end of the age is reached, but it has influence and leaves fruits, for eternity.

It stands to reason that if all things were created by Christ and for Him (*Col. 1:16*) then what was created was good, and enduring. And whatever the 'reconciliation' of the creation may mean in exact terms, it appears to imply that there is to be a 'carry-over' of the first creation into the new order of things to be inaugurated at the second coming of Christ.

A further piece of evidence for the 'carry over' of the effects of the Christian's calling in this life to the world to come are the references in the New Testament to heaven as a city (*Heb. 13:14, Rev. 21*). In 'The Task' William Cowper wrote that

God made the country, and man made the town:
What wonder then, that health and virtue, gifts
That can alone make sweet the bitter draught
That life holds out to all, should most abound
And least be threatened in the fields and groves?

Such lines reflect Cowper's own preference for rural life, and no doubt there is some truth in them as they refer to the towns of the eighteenth century or of today. But the first line of the quotation is hardly a biblical emphasis, for the teaching of Scripture is that the work of God will be consummated in a city, the New Jerusalem.

The difficulties encountered in thinking about the life to come are so very great because human knowledge is dim and partial. What exactly does Paul mean by a 'spiritual body'? How is the church to enjoy the presence of Christ? What will the life in heaven be like? What sort of a city is heaven? How is the symbolism to be understood? Many such questions press upon the believer, and yet these difficulties in thought ought not to be exaggerated. To begin with, there are the general assurances of Scripture regarding the presence of Christ, freedom from sin, and glad and joyful service. Christian faith is able to rely and to rest content upon these. And while the fragmentary character of our present knowledge is obvious, as it was obvious to the early church (*1 Cor. 13.12*), nevertheless it is *real* knowledge. There *is* a life to come, a life of freedom from sin and sorrow to be lived in the presence of Christ. While the biblical imagery of a city with streets of gold is clearly symbolic it is nonetheless appropriate symbolism, intended to convey as much of the truth as it is either possible or useful to know now. So we must conclude that a city is a better symbol than a factory or a farm, and gold than tin or chalk. It is not sufficient to say that this is 'spiritual' symbolism, any more than it is satisfactory to say that it is 'mythical'. The words are intended to convey *realities*.

And so whatever the exact character of heaven is to be the biblical model of it as a city must accurately reflect that. A city is a complex social organism and organisation in which people co-operate using their different skills. It has the benefits of political rule. Is it conceivable that the personalities of the heavenly citizens will have been partly formed by their service as earthly citizens, that they will bear some positive relationship to the manner and faithfulness with which they have carried out their daily callings? Indeed, is it conceivable that heaven should *not* bear this character? Purged from sin and glorified, will not the people of God have the personalities they very largely had on earth?

But there is further evidence yet. The biblical teaching is that a person's calling is in obedience to the original cultural mandate to replenish the earth and subdue it. Due to sin this mandate has never been fully carried out, but to the extent that it is carried out properly there are products of such activity – in practical crafts, in arts and sciences – which will also figure in that new creation for which the old creation groans (*Rom. 8:22*). For is it likely that the potential which is unlocked from the creation as the result of the common grace of God operating in human culture, to which the Christian contributes as he carries out his daily calling, is confined only to this present world? Is it thinkable that the potential unlocked from God's good creation in the course of time should be abandoned in eternity? Certainly the earth will be transformed by purging fire, as Peter informs us (*2 Peter 3:13*). But is it conceivable that the new earth should bear no relationship to the old? Part of the significance of the creation being pronounced good by its Creator at the first (*Gen. 1:31*) is that such cultural activity as is in accordance with the will and plan of God will endure the fire.

To raise such questions is not to speculate idly but to attempt to work out the implications of biblical teaching to the limit and so to profit by every word that has proceeded out of God's mouth. If such suggestions are along the right lines, then this indicates that the thought of the Christian's life as a calling has importance not only for this life but for the life to come. For while the life to come is one of unimaginable fulness and blessing, nevertheless in that life the redeemed are still people, human characters, whose personalities have been formed during and through their earthly pilgrimage, and who, though judged and transformed, are still in a substantial sense the people that they were. Such an emphasis invites Christians to place a much more positive emphasis upon the abiding significance of their daily callings than they are accustomed to do.

CONCLUSION

This book has had a modest aim, to recall and re-emphasise the biblical and Reformation teaching about the daily vocation of Christians. Highlighting this teaching will not solve any problems. It is certainly not a panacea, a magic wand to wave in front of difficulties and duties to make them vanish. In some ways, recognising one's calling is only a beginning, but it does at least give a Christian a perspective from which he may strive to see his entire life as integrated in the service of the Lord. Much hard thinking remains to be done as each Christian works out for himself not only what it means to be effectually called by divine grace, called to liberty in Christ, but also what it means to glorify God in his daily calling with heaven in prospect.

General Index

Index of Scripture References

Index